Christians and Muslims
Race To Do Good

MESSAGES FROM THE HOLY BIBLE & THE HOLY QUR'AN

By Major Afzaal Shafi

1

Published by Major Afzaal Shafi
Hope, Castle Cavendish Works
Dorking Road, Radford, Nottingham
NG7 5NP England

Email. admin@racetodogood.co.uk
Website: www.racetodogood.co.uk

British Library Catalogue in Publication Data
A catalogue record for this book is available from the British
Library.

ISBN 978-0-9568544-0-7

Contents

4

About the Author

Major Afzaal was born in Pakistan, served in the Pakistan Army as an officer and retired at the rank of Major. He is a war veteran, operated behind enemy lines in Indian occupied Kashmir as a Commando office during 1971 war, where he was declared missing believed killed. However he returned to his homeland as a Ghazi and was recommended for a bravery award of Sitara-Jurat for leading the highly risky and successful commando operations.

Major Afzaal is a double graduate from the University of Punjab, Lahore (Pakistan), and Pakistan Army Staff College (Quetta). He has lived in Great Britain since 1984 and has been a Mortgage Adviser. He has three sons and a daughter who are also living a happy life in the UK.

Based upon the research from the Holy Bible and the Holy Qur'an, in this book Major Afzaal urges the Christians and Muslims of Great Britain to lead the world in a race to do good. This is to reach out to the weak, helpless, in pain and victims of our world, regardless of race, religion, colour or gender, to follow the strive and struggle of Jesus and Muhammad (peace be upon both of them).

Introduction

Islam is the only non Christian faith which has in its article of faith that, NO MUSLIM IS A MUSLIM UNLESS HE BELIEVES IN JESUS CHRIST (Peace Be Upon Him)

I have chosen the title of my book from the Holy Qur'an, which reveals that the Jews, Christians and Muslims **'race to do good.'** The Christians and Muslims are the two biggest religions, which brings them an additional responsibility to lead the world and work together and try to establish peace and justice for all, regardless of race, religion, colour or gender. I start with three verses on the subject revealed in the Holy Qur'an, a glimpse of Jesus' teachings from the Holy Bible, and a very small passage from the last Sermon of Prophet Muhammad (peace be upon both of them).

*We have prescribed a law and path to each of you. If God had so willed, He would have made you all one community, but He desired to test you in different ways through that which He has given to you, so **race to do good**. You will all return to God and He will make clear to you the matters you used to dispute about. **(Qur'an 5:48)***

*'Each community has its own direction to which it turns its face; **race to do good** and wherever you are, God will bring you all together'. **(Qur'an 2:148)***

*You are sure to find of all the people, the nearest in friendship to the Muslims are those who say; 'We are Christians'. **(Qur'an 5:82)***

The best guideline about equality of human rights, respect and regards for the whole of humanity can be attributed to Jesus and Muhammad (peace be upon them).

Jesus said, Golden Rule. *"In everything do to others as you would have them do to you; for **this is the law and the prophets.**" (Matthew 7:12)* '

The Last Sermon of Prophet Muhammad[(PBUH)] He said (in brief), "hurt no one so that no one may hurt you. All mankind are from Adam and Eve, a white has no superiority over a black, nor a black has any superiority over white, **except by piety and good deeds**.

Human beings ever since their existence have been curious to find the answers of some basic questions like: Where did I come from? Why I am here? Where do I go from here? What is the purpose of my life? Why the Jews, Christians and Muslims believe what they believe? In order to find the answers to these questions, I will take you through many verses of the **Holy Qur'an and the Holy Bible.**

The message of friendship between the Muslims and Christians is revealed in the Holy Qur'an. Maybe God has blessed the Muslims and Christians to work together, to establish peace and justice for all in our world before the second coming of Jesus [(PBUH)] they both believe in.

The very first revelation of the Holy Qur'an starts with, 'Read, Recite and Proclaim in the name of your Lord who created you.' The question arises as to, 'what to proclaim and how to proclaim.' In an attempt to answer this question I carried out a successful trial to proclaim to some Christians, and also had the views of some Muslims. I have recommended a **Four Step Guide** to proclaim under the guidance of the

Holy Qur'an, which can be a very good exercise for mutual understanding, if you get it right. This book is addressed to the Christians and Muslims to help the dialogue between them.

Surely, it will take your breath away, when you read in my book about Jesus and Muhammad (peace be upon both of them), both in the Bible and the Qur'an, about their prophecies, their strive and struggle in support of victims. Church is very important to Christians, but I am choosing to concentrate on Jesus (PBUH) only as he appears in the Holy Bible and the Holy Qur'an.

Offering prayers in the church or mosque but to do evil deeds as a way of life is a deceptive appearance, i.e. **'façade' (Matthew 6:5,6 and Qur'an 29:2,4, 107:4-7).** God knows our intentions and will judge us by our deeds and not only by our duty of prayers. Indeed, the good deeds being mindful of God are the essence of worship and the purpose of our life. I urge the Christians and the Muslims of Great Britain, to lead the world in a **race to do good.**

Note. I have provided the extracts from the New Revised Standard Version of the Bible. However, I have not provided the word by word translation of the verse/verses of the Qur'an in this book; instead I have given the spirit of the messages, to make it easy for you to understand. In order to provide you with the overall context of each message, I have supported it with many other verses where required, rather than a verse on its own which can be misleading.

- The interviewees' names have not been disclosed to protect their identities.

Ancient World, Before the Revealed Religions

Let me take you on an exciting journey back in time to about 3500 BC. We will examine how humans were living, what their beliefs were and what effect the beliefs had on them. We will also examine whether the revealed religions have solved the problems of humanity, or due to the lack of awareness of their followers, it has become the source of the problems? The history of the ancient world tells us that the people were on the move in search of food for survival; however they had the most important benefit of a simple and small family life with an absolute freedom of mind, with no stress, and had all the time to explore, laugh and enjoy nature.

In the Qur'an 13:38 and 35:24, it is revealed that the messengers and the Scriptures have been sent by God to all the people in all ages with the same message, to worship One God, and believe in the Last Day. However, history tells us that they used to worship many gods, and they had the belief about the life hereafter. About 10,000 BC, in the Middle East, the tribes of Somer invented the first ever farming method, which quickly spread to the rest of the world and humans no longer needed to be on the move and started to live a settled life as a community in the villages and towns. The settled life as a community gave birth to the power and control by the bullies and powerful. They invented a clever and crooked method of being self-appointed representatives of many gods on the earth to control the minds of the people, to exercise power. The common man was reduced to serving their god's representative, while the kings, along with their priests and other supporters (hypocrites), had the best of everything. Kings built huge palaces for themselves, raised their armies and embarked upon conquering each other to bring wealth to their land and to expand their empires.

The kings married unlimited numbers of wives, and to ensure that their god's blood was not diluted, they married their own sisters and had children from their sister wives only. The eldest son was to inherit the throne to continue with the same practice for future generations. The Bible tells us that the men used to keep their beautiful daughters for themselves, and used to kill their children as offerings to their gods. The kings were buried in the tombs with their belongings and also with their servants to serve them in the life hereafter.

The Indian sub-continent had and still continues with the caste system in their Hindu belief, that the humans are born as superior or inferior, which was apparently an administrative arrangement and a solution to run the society during that time. The Arabs invented a clever method of worshipping their many gods at Kaba in Mecca, absolutely naked without wearing any clothes, and justified their reasons that they were born without clothes so their gods would be best pleased.

Creator in the Light of Science

The Universe

Let us have a look as a lay man and woman at the discoveries of science in the field of the universe. It is estimated that the universe contains billions of galaxies, and our milky way is one of these galaxies. There are billions of stars in the Milky Way and our sun is just one of those. It is estimated that in order to travel out of our galaxy, it will take about 100,000 years travelling at the speed of light. We, the humans are just tiny creatures, but each of us is a very special creature to the Creator as per the Holy Books. Where do we get this knowledge from? Obviously our Creator has given us the intellect and ingenuity to explore this world, so it can be attributed to the Creator. The Creator has also given us signs in the Holy Book of the Qur'an to explore the world and to find it to be true. Besides the knowledge, the Creator has provided all the blessings that His creatures need to live. It is simply beyond the imagination of humans about the extent of this universe and it makes it even impossible to imagine about the Creator who created this universe, except that He is the most supreme. We can see Him through everything that exists, although we cannot see Him physically. It makes us look so small a creature living on a very small part of the universe, with neither control over our own life and death nor upon the behaviour of our planet that we live on. The science therefore goes to prove that there is a God who created this universe, created us, rules and controls our world, and He is the lord, our God.

How small we are

The science tells us that if we pick up some soil on a shovel, there is about four times more bacteria in that soil than the number of humans in our world. This is for us to realise just how small we are in the universe even if someone is holding the highest office. No religion can claim that they have completely understood God, but we can be very close to God by being mindful of God and doing good deeds, because He sees us in secret.

Construction of child in mother's womb

Let us have a look at the very basic knowledge of science about ourselves as a common man and woman. The development of a child in the mother's womb is a continuous process, which starts from a single cell, when the male sperm and female egg join together. This one cell, by a multiplying and copying process, forms into trillions of cells of the embryo. Each cell performs a perfect function to ensure proper and progressive development of the embryo, starting with the brain. Many cells form the hands, and at some stage some of them commit suicide to make empty spaces to become the gaps between the fingers of the child. It is believed that the length of the vein system of the child is approximately equal to the circumference of the earth. The eyes are the most amazing camera to perfection, which consists of so many components.

Only recently scientists have confirmed the order of development of hearing and seeing in a child, which was revealed by the Qur'an, that the first of the senses is hearing, followed by the sight.

And God has brought you out from the wombs of your mother while you know nothing. And He gave you hearing, sight and mind that you might give thanks. **(Qur'an 16:78)**

It is He who created you. He gave you hearing, sight and understanding---. **(Qur'an 67:23)**

Until recently, it was thought that the bones form at the same time as the muscles, but the latest research has discovered the truth, previously revealed in the Qur'an that science was not aware of. The Qur'an revealed the stages of the development of a child. We all know that the first human, 'Adam,' God created from the clay. The Qur'an 23:12-14, has revealed in these verses, the various stages of the child in mother's womb. The first stage is where the drop of fluid from the male is placed in the female's womb. The drop is formed into a clot of congealed blood, which is a leach-like substance that clings to the mother's womb. Like a clinging leach feeds, so does the child from the mother. The clot is then formed into a lump of flesh, which develops into bones. Then, the bones are covered with the flesh, which science has discovered only recently. Science has also been amazed to discover the revelation in the Qur'an that, this is the stage where another creature of a human child comes into being. However the Qur'an further reveals the stage where the life comes into being 'by breathing a spirit into the child,' which we all know happens, but science does not know how it happens, who breathes a spirit into the child? The science was not aware of the fact that the gender of the child depends upon the sperm of the father. People in the past used to blame the women for giving birth to a girl. Even Henry VIII blamed his wife for giving birth to a girl and not a boy who could inherit his throne. He wanted to divorce his wife to marry another woman to have a son. As a matter of fact, if someone had to be blamed, it was appropriate for Henry to blame himself. However, the Qur'an 53:45,46, revealed 1400 years ago, 'He created two sexes, male and female, from the drop of sperm when ejected.' Just imagine if there was no good balance of the sex of male and female children born in our world. Who is controlling this crucial balance? It is fair to conclude from this knowledge that, to supervise trillions of cells of a child in a mother's womb is a much more complicated task, as compared to **monitor the deeds** of each person, which is revealed in the Qur'an 13: 8,11, that there are guardian angels watching over each person.

O people! It is you who need God; He alone is self sufficient, and praiseworthy. **(Qur'an 35:15)**

The life of this world is nothing but an amusement and diversion; the true life is hereafter. **(Qur'an 29:64)**

Remember, the Day when We roll up the skies like a writer rolls up his scrolls. We shall reproduce the creation as We began the first creation. **(Qur'an 21:104)**

In view of the above, it is fair to ask: Who gives us the life? Who controls our life? Who monitors our life? He is the Lord, our God. It is we, who need Him during this short life, which is only an amusement and diversion, and it is He whom we will all return to.

Background History of the Revealed Religions

It is important to know about the time period related to the three revealed religions. The time period of Abraham was 1800 BC, Moses 1400 BC, David 1000 BC, and Muhammad about 600 AD (peace be upon all of them).

The Holy Bible tells us that Abraham [(PBUH)] was a man of faith with complete devotion to God. The Lord came to Abraham in a vision, 'And he brought him outside and said, "Look towards heaven, and number the stars, if you are able to number them." Then he said to him, "So shall your offspring be."' And he believed the Lord, and he counted it to him as righteousness' (Genesis 15:1,5,6). The Lord God made a covenant with Abraham that He will raise prophets from his offspring, including the son of Hagar because he is also your offspring.

> But God said to Abraham, "...*for it is through Isaac that offspring shall be named for you. As for the son of the slave woman, I will make a nation of him also, because he is your offspring."* **(Genesis 21:12- 13)**

As per the family tree in the Bible, Abraham had his first son Ishmael from his wife Hagar and another son Isaac from his wife Sarah. Moses was a descendent from Isaac and Abraham. David was descended from Moses, Isaac and Abraham. Jesus was born miraculously without a father from the virgin mother Mary and her husband Joseph was descended from David, Isaac and Abraham. Muhammad

15

was a descendent from Kedar, Ishmael and Abraham (peace be upon all of them). **(Genesis 25:13)**.

God fulfilled His promise by sending prophets from the descendants of Abraham and revealed the Holy Books, the Torah to Moses, Psalms to David, the Gospels to Jesus and the Qur'an to Muhammad (peace be upon all of them).

Abraham ^(PBUH) is revered in the Holy Bible and the Holy Qur'an and his special relationship with God is emphasised. All the three religions consider Abraham as their father in faith (complete devotion to God).

Judaism

> Now the Lord said to Abram, *"Go from your country and your kindred and your father's house to the land that I will show you. I will make of you a great nation, and I will bless you, and make your name great, so that you will be a blessing. I will bless those who bless you, and the one who curses you I will curse; and in you all the families of the earth shall be blessed." **(Genesis 12:1-3)***

Christianity
The traditional view of Christianity is that, the promise made to Abraham in Genesis 12 above is that, through Abraham's seed all the people of the earth would be blessed, which has been fulfilled through Jesus as Abraham's seed. For the promise, that, 'He should be heir of the world,' was not to Abraham or to his seed through the law but through the righteousness of faith (Galatians 3:7,29, and Romans 4:13).

Islam

"God took Abraham as close friend. We gave him Isaac and Jacob and guided them as We guided Noah and of his offspring David, Solomon, Job, Joseph, Moses and Aaron. We guided Zachariah, John, Jesus, and Elijah. And We guided some of their forefathers, their offspring and their brothers. We chose them and guided on a straight path." **(Qur'an 4:125, 6:84-87)**

Abraham [PBUH] and his sons are counted amongst prophets and God sent the revelations to them.

"Verily O Prophet, We have sent revelation to you as We sent to Noah and the prophets who came after him, to Abraham, Ishmael, Isaac, Jacob, and the tribes, to Jesus, Job, Jonah, Aaron, and Solomon, and We gave David the Book Zabur (Psalms). Also to other Apostles mentioned before and also to some We have not mentioned. God spoke directly to Moses. We sent all these Apostles with good news and warning so that people are left with no excuse before God." **(Qur'an 4:163-165)**

"In the matters of faith, He has decreed for you the same commandment that He gave Noah, which We have revealed to you and which We enjoined on Abraham and Moses and Jesus: "Establish this faith and do not divide into factions within it." **(Qur'an 42:13)**

Lineage. Abraham and Isaac leads to Moses and to Jerusalem. Abraham, Isaac and David leads to Jesus and to Jerusalem. Abraham and Ishmael leads to Muhammad and to Mecca [PBUT].

The Fundamental Differences Between Judaism, Christianity and Islam

Let us have a look at the fundamental differences between these three religions, and try to find out if there is any chance of them coming together or will they have to learn to differ?

Judaism
The Jews have a faith of Abraham (complete devotion to God) which was confirmed to be the same when God spoke direct to Moses, and gave ten commandments, 'you shall have no other gods before me, you shall not make yourself an idol, you shall not make wrongful use of the name of the Lord your God, remember the sabbath day, and keep it holy, honour your father and your mother, you shall not murder, you shall not commit adultery, you shall not steal, you shall not bear false witness, you shall not covet'. (Exodus 20)

The Jews believe that a true prophet must accomplish two basic requirements. He must believe in one God, and must not change the divine law (or Torah), which was given to them when God spoke direct to Moses. Anyone coming to change the Torah is immediately rejected as a prophet (Deuteronomy 13:1-4). The Jews therefore do not recognise both Jesus and Muhammad [PBUT] as prophets.

In order for someone to claim that, he is the true Messiah, he must fulfil four of many other conditions given below.

1. *Build the third temple. (Ezekiel 37:26-28)*
2. *Gather all the Jews back to the land of Israel. (Isaiah 43:5-6)*
3. *Usher in the era of world peace and end all hatred, oppression, suffering and disease. As it says, 'Nation shall not lift up sword against nation, neither shall they learn war anymore.'* **(Isaiah 2:4)**
4. *Spread universal message of God of Israel, which will unite humanity as one. As it says, 'And the Lord will become king over all the earth; on that day the Lord will be one and his name one.'* **(Isaiah 2:4, Zechariah 14:9)**

All past claims, including Jesus of Nazareth [PBUH] have been rejected by the Jews on the above grounds. The Jews are still waiting for the Messiah to come. The Messiah must fulfil the prophecies outright, and that there is no concept of the second coming according to Jewish interpretation of the Scripture.

The records of the Holy Bible. Prophet Moses [PBUH] had shown his grave concerns about the Scribes corrupting the Holy Scripture Deut 31:25-29, and after about eight hundred years, the Prophet Jeremiah [PBUH] confirmed it as per the below extracts of the Holy Bible.

How can you say, *"We are wise, and the law of the Lord is with us",* when, in fact, the false pen of the scribes has made it into a lie? **(Jeremiah 8:8)**

Christianity
Christian belief is based upon the fulfilment of the prophecies about Jesus written in the law of Moses, the

prophets and the Psalms, hundreds of years before the birth of Jesus. They believe that God visited our world in the human form of Jesus. Christians believe in one God, the God of Moses but worship trinity (God the Father, the Son and the Holy Spirit), three characteristics of one God (source www.christianity.org.uk). They believe that Jesus is the Messiah, and that all the prophecies about the Messiah have been fulfilled through Jesus, and that Jesus will come again (for all humanity) to judge the living and the dead.

The Christians believe that,

'No one has ever seen God. It is God the only Son, who is close to the Father's heart, who has made him known', **(John 1:18)**.

And they believe in Jesus, as the first and the last, the beginning and the end,

'I am the Alpha and the Omega, the first and the last, the beginning and the end'. **(Revelations 22:13)**

The Christians believe in the previous revelations and the prophets, and the Last Day. They regard Abraham [(PBUH)], the father of their faith (complete devotion to God). They believe that the salvation for all the people of our world can only be achieved through the belief in Jesus, son of God, who died for our sins as per the fulfilment of the prophecies about Jesus. [(PBUH)] The Cross, crucifixion and resurrection are central to their belief. The details of the prophecies in the Old Testament of the Bible and their fulfilment in the New Testament of the Bible are given under the heading, 'About Christianity.'

Islam

The prophecies about the coming of Muhammad [(PBUH)] are prescribed both in the Old Testament and New Testament of the Bible, hundreds of years before his birth. God fulfilled His promise by raising Muhammad [(PBUH)] a prophet from the offspring of Abraham, and revealed the Qur'an as the last and final revelation of God. The details of the prophecies and their fulfilment are given under the heading, 'About Islam.' The Muslims have a faith of Abraham [(PBUH)] and believe in the Last Day. They believe in the previous revelations and the previous prophets, and believe in the Holy Qur'an as the last and final revelation from God, and Muhammad [(PBUH)], the last and final prophet. Anyone claims to be a prophet after Muhammad [(PBUH)], he and his followers are not Muslims as per the Holy Qur'an.

The concept of God revealed in the Holy Qur'an.

'Say, 'He is God, God the eternal. He begot none nor was He begotten. There is nothing like Him'. **(Qur'an 112:1-4)**

The Holy Qur'an 5:43-48, reveals for the People of Book (Jews and Christians), to follow their own religions revealed in their Holy Books which are guidance and light, the distinction between right and wrong for them, however the records in the Holy Bible are not preserved as revealed. It is also revealed for the Jews, Christians and Muslims that, race to do good, you will all return to God and He will make clear to you the matters you used to dispute about. However many Muslims have been made to believe that, Islam is the only religion acceptable to God.

Muslims believe that Jesus [(PBUH)] was the most miraculous prophet, a Messiah, he was born miraculously without any male intervention and he healed those born blind, or were ill with leprosy and gave life to the dead, with God's permission. The Holy Qur'an denies that Jesus is divine, or God incarnate. It also denies the Christian idea of God, understood and known as Father, Son and Holy Spirit, often called trinity. It is also revealed that Jesus was neither killed, nor crucified, it was made to appear like that to them, God raised him up to Himself. The Muslims and Christians though both believe in Jesus as a Messiah, raised by God to Himself and the second coming of Jesus, but with major differences.

In view of the above, I can summarise that there is hardly any chance of these three religions coming together, to believe in each other's religion. The question arises that, though they may not believe in each other, can they live peacefully with the differences, learn to differ, and demonstrate mutual respect and dignity for each other? Can they live peacefully within their own factions? **Maybe, they are all being tested, whether they prefer God's consciousness, to love all His creatures and the environment, or fall into the trap of Satan, the devil?**

About Christianity

Let us see why Christians believe what they believe. Holy Bible! About Jesus! (PBUH) The purpose of life of the Christians! The prophecies about Jesus and their fulfilment through Jesus! Disputed prophecies between the Jews, Christians and Muslims! Holy Qur'an about Christianity!

Holy Bible

The Holy Bible is a collection of books written over a time span of around 1500 years. It consists of the Old Testament (before Jesus), and the New Testament (after Jesus). While Jews follow only the Old Testament (also known as the Hebrew Bible), for Christians both testaments reflect and serve as a source for Christian theology.

The Christians' belief is based upon the fulfilment of the prophecies about Jesus written in the Law of Moses, the prophets and the Psalms, hundreds of years before the birth of Jesus. They believe that God visited our world as was revealed in the prophecies and fulfilled through Jesus. They believe in one God, associate no partners with Him and worship none but Him alone, but worship trinity (God the Father, the Son and the Holy Spirit), which are three characteristics of one and the same God.* The crucifixion, the Cross and resurrection are central to their belief. They believe in Abraham(PBUH) as the father of their faith (complete devotion to God).

*www.christianity.org.uk

The New Testament consists of 27 Books. The four Gospels, 'Matthew, Mark, Luke and John,' consists of narratives of the life, teachings, death, and resurrection of Jesus. Other Books are as below:

Acts of Apostles. These are referred as the 'Acts,' the narratives of the Apostles ministry after Jesus' death and resurrection.

Pauline Letters. These were the letters written in the name of Apostle Paul to Christians in different cities to address issues faced by different communities. It includes, Letter to Romans, first and second Letter to Corinthians, Letter to Galatians, Letter to Ephesians, Letter to Colossians, first and second Letter to Thessalonians, and Letter to Philemon.

Pastoral Letters. These were letters addressed to individuals with Pastoral oversight of churches, and addresses issues of Christian living, doctrine and leadership. It includes first and second Letter to Timothy, and Letter to Titus.

Catholic Letters. These are both letters and treaties written to churches. It includes James, 1Peter, 2Peter, 1John, 2John, 3John, and Jude (brother of Jesus).

Hebrews. The author of the Letter to the Hebrew is anonymous.

The Revelation to John. This is the final Book of the New Testament, believed to be written by John, Jesus' disciple. It describes a vision John received from Jesus Christ. It opens with letters to seven churches and thereafter takes the form of an 'Apocalypse.'

About Jesus (PBUH)

Jesus' birth was unique from the virgin mother Mary, without any male intervention.

Jesus was unique, to be blessed by God with the Holy Spirit.

Jesus' mission was unique, only for about three years. He did not marry, and had no children.

Jesus' miracles were unique, giving life to dead, curing born blind and lepers.

Jesus' teachings were unique in the form of parables while he spoke to the people.

Jesus' departure from this world was unique which has left an everlasting impression on the minds and hearts of all humans for all times to come.

Jesus' second coming in this world will be unique, which keeps us all in waiting and in suspense.

May God bless his soul in peace for his spiritual teachings for the humanity at the cost of his sufferings, in the hands of the Jews and Romans till he was raised up by God to Himself, hence the Scripture was fulfilled, but it is not all over, we have to wait for his second coming.

Prophecies about Jesus (PBUH)

The details of the prophecies (Old Testament) and their fulfilment (New Testament) of the Bible are separately given below:

Will be a descendent of Abraham's son Isaac (Genesis 17:21), descendant of Judah (not of the other 11 brothers of Jacob), of the house of David (2 Samuel 7:12-16, Jeremiah 23:5, Psalm 89:3-4). Fulfilled (Matthew 1, Luke 1:27,32,69, 3:23-38).

The Sceptre shall not depart from Judah, until the Messiah comes (Genesis 49:10). Fulfilled, The Genealogy of Jesus Christ, son of Amminadab, son of Admin, son of Arni, son of Hezron, son of Perez, son of Judah (Luke 3:33).

Will be born of a virgin (Isaiah 7:14). Fulfilled (Luke 1:31-33).

Will be born in the city of Bethlehem (Ephratah) (Micah 5:2). Fulfilled (Luke 2:4-7).

Will be a Priest after the order of Melchisedek (Psalm 110:4). Fulfilled (Hebrews 5:6), as he says also in another place, 'You are a priest forever, according to the order of Melchizedek.'

Will come while the Temple of Jerusalem is standing (Malachi 3:1, Psalm 118:26). Fulfilled, 'Then Jesus entered the temple and drove out all who were selling and buying in the temple, and he overturned the tables of the money changers and the seats of those who sold doves' (Matthew 21:12).

Will perform many miracles (Isaiah 35:5-6). Will open the eyes of the blind (Isaiah 29:18). Fulfilled (Matthew 9:27-31, 12:22, 20:29, Mark 8:22-26, Luke 11:14,18, John 9:1-7).

Will speak in parables (Psalm 78:2). Fulfilled, Jesus told the crowds all these things in parables; without a parable he told them nothing (Matthew 13:34).

His own people (Jews) will reject him, while the gentile (non Jews) will believe in him (Isaiah 8:14, 28:16, 49:6, 50:6,

60:3, Psalms 22:7,8, 118:22). Fulfilled, 'To you then who believe, he is precious; but for those who do not believe, "The stone that the builders rejected has become the very head of the corner" **(1Peter 2:7)**.

A Messenger (a man of the wilderness) will prepare the way for him (Isaiah 40:3, Malachi 3:1). Fulfilled (Matthew 3:1-3, 11,10, John 1:23, Luke 1:17) (about John the Baptist)). 'With the spirit and power of Elijah he will go before him, to turn the hearts of parents to their children, and the disobedient to the wisdom of the righteous, to make ready a people prepared for the Lord' **(Luke 1:17, also Matthew 3:1-3,11,10 and John 1:23)**.

Will enter Jerusalem riding on a donkey (Zachariah 9:9) Fulfilled, 'Tell the daughter of Zion, Look, your king is coming to you, humble, and mounted on a donkey, and on a colt, the foal of a donkey' **(Matthew 21:5, also Luke 19:32-37)**.

Will be betrayed by a friend, the price of his betrayal will be 30 pieces of silver, which will be cast onto the floor of the Temple and will be used to buy a potter's field (Psalm 41:9, Zachariah 11:12,13). Fulfilled (Matthew 26:47,48, 27:3-10).

Crucifixion foretold **(Psalm 22)**.

*For dogs are all around me; a company of evildoers encircles me. My hands and feet have shrivelled; I can count all my bones. They stare and gloat over me; they divide my clothes among themselves, and for my clothing they cast lots. **(Psalm 22:16-18)**. Fulfilled **(Matthew 27:26-30,46, Galatians 3:13)***

Will not open his mouth to defend himself (Isaiah 53:7).

*He was oppressed, and he was afflicted, yet he did not open his mouth; like a lamb that is led to the slaughter, and like a sheep that before its shearers is silent, so he did not open his mouth. By a perversion of justice he was taken away. Who could have imagined his future? For he was cut off from the land of the living, stricken for the transgression of my people. They made his grave with the wicked and his tomb with the rich, although he had done no violence, and there was no deceit in his mouth. **(Isaiah 53:7-9)***

Will be revealed to Israel, but He would then 'be cut off, but not for himself' **(Daniel 9:26)**. Fulfilled, **(Matthew 27:12)**, 'But when he was accused by the chief priests and elders, he did not answer'.

Will be beaten and spit upon (Isaiah 50:6). Fulfilled (Matthew 27:30).

They will divide and cast lots for his clothing (Psalms 22:18). Fulfilled (Matthew 27:35).

Will be 'numbered with the transgressors' **(Isaiah 53:12)**. Fulfilled (Matthew 27:38), crucified as a criminal in between two thieves).

His hands and feet will be pierced (Zachriah 12:10, Psalms 22:16). Fulfilled (Galatians 3:13).

He will be given sour wine to drink (Psalm 69:21). Fulfilled (Matthew 27:34).

His bones will not be broken (Psalms 34:20, Exodus 12:46). Fulfilled (John 19:33).

He will say, "My God, My God, why hast thou forsaken me?" **(Psalm 22:1)**. Fulfilled (Matthew 27:46).

He will be buried with the rich/wicked (Isaiah 53:9). Fulfilled (Matthew 27:57-61).

He will not decay, and will be resurrected from the dead (Psalm 16:10). Fulfilled (Acts 2:31).

He will ascend into heaven (Psalm 68:18). Fulfilled (Hebrews 1:3).

He will be the Son of God (Psalm 2:7). Fulfilled **(Matthew 3:17)**, 'And a voice from heaven said, "This is my Son, the Beloved, with whom I am well pleased."'

Resurrection of Jesus (PBUH)
The prophecies about the resurrection of Jesus are written in the Old Testament of the Bible as per the interpretations of the Christians (Psalms 16:10, 40:2,3, 49:15, Hosea 6:2, and Zachariah 12:10, as below).

> *And I will pour out on the house of David and the inhabitants of Jerusalem, a spirit of grace and supplication. They will look on me for one they have pierced, and they will mourn for Him as one mourns for an only child.* ***(Zachariah 12:10)***

God raised up Jesus (PBUH) **to Himself**

> *The Lord says to my lord, "Sit at my right hand until I make your enemies your footstool."* ***(Psalm 110:1)***.

Fulfilled. *'This Jesus God raised up, and of that all of us are witnesses. Being therefore exalted at the right hand of God, and having received from the Father the promise of the Holy Spirit, he has poured out this that you both see and hear.'* **(Acts 2:32,33)**

Fulfilment of Prophecies about Jesus ^(PBUH)

Birth of Jesus Foretold
In the sixth month the angel Gabriel was sent by God to a town in Galilee called Nazareth, to a virgin engaged to a man whose name was Joseph, of the house of David. The virgin's name was Mary. The angel said to her, "Do not be afraid, Mary, for you have found favour with God. And now, you will conceive in your womb and bear a son, and you will name him Jesus. He will be great, and will be called the Son of the Most High, and the Lord God will give to him the throne of his ancestor David. He will reign over the house of Jacob forever, and of his kingdom there will be no end." Mary said to the angel, "How can this be, since I am a virgin?" The angel said to her, "The Holy Spirit will come upon you, and the power of the Most High will overshadow you; therefore the child to be born will be holy; he will be called Son of God" **(Luke 1:26,30-35)**.

The Birth of Jesus Christ ^(PBUH)
In those days a decree went out from Emperor Augustus that all the world should be registered. Joseph also went from the town of Nazareth in Galilee to Judea, to the city of David called Bethlehem, because he was descended from the house and family of David. He went to be registered with Mary, to whom he was engaged and who was expecting a

child. While they were there, the time came for her to deliver her child. And she gave birth to her firstborn son and wrapped him in bands of cloth, and laid him in a manger, because there was no place for them in the inn **(Luke 2:1,4-7)**.

Miracles of Jesus (PBUH)

Jesus started his ministry at the age of 30, with 12 disciples. He performed many miracles to include giving life to the dead, cure born blind and lepers, heal others in need, and turning water into wine. His teachings to the people were in parables as revealed in the prophecies (see under the teachings of Jesus). Then his disciples asked him what this parable meant. He said, "To you it has been given to know the secrets of the kingdom of God; but to others I speak in parables, so that "looking they may not perceive, and listening they may not understand."

The Triumphal Entry

After he had said this, he went on ahead, going up to Jerusalem. Then they brought it to Jesus; and after throwing their cloaks on the colt, they set Jesus on it. As he rode along, people kept spreading their cloaks on the road. As he was now approaching the path down from the Mount of Olives, the whole multitude of the disciples began to praise God joyfully with a loud voice for all the deeds of power that they had seen, saying, "Blessed is the king who comes in the name of the Lord! Peace in heaven, and glory in the highest heaven!" Some of the Pharisees in the crowd said to him, "Teacher, order your disciples to stop." He answered, "I tell you, if these were silent, the stones would shout out."

Jesus ^(PBUH) Foretold about Crucifixion

When Jesus had finished saying all these things, he said to his disciples, "You know that after two days the Passover is coming, and the Son of Man will be handed over to be crucified."

Betrayal and Arrest of Jesus ^(PBUH)

The chief priest and the scribes were threatened of Jesus' teachings, because he was critical of Jews' interpretation of the Law of Moses, and they made a plot to kill Jesus. Judas was one of the 12 disciples who betrayed Jesus, as Jesus had foretold during the Last Supper besides the above prophecy. While he was still speaking, suddenly a crowd came, and the one called Judas, one of the 12, was leading them. He approached Jesus to kiss him; but Jesus said to him, "Judas, is it with a kiss that you are betraying the Son of Man?" Jesus was arrested and delivered to the high priest and the elders in Jerusalem.

Judas Hangs Himself

When Jesus was later condemned, Judas repented, and went to the temple to return 30 pieces of silver to the chief priests and elders, which he had received a price for betrayal. He said to them that, "I have sinned by betraying innocent blood." Throwing down the pieces of silver on the floor of the temple, he departed, and he went and hanged himself. The chief priest said it is not lawful to put this money into the treasury, since it is blood money. After conferring, they used that money to buy the potter's field to bury foreigners. For this reason that field has been called the Field of Blood to this day (Matthew 26:47,48, 27:3-10).

Jesus (PBUH) Before Caiaphas and the Council

Those who had seized Jesus led him to Caiaphas the high priest, where the scribes and elders had gathered. Two witnesses said, "This fellow said, 'I am able to destroy the temple of God and to build it in three days.'" The high priest stood up and said, "Have you no answer? What is it that they testify against you?" But Jesus was silent. Then the high priest said to him, "I put you under oath before the living God, tell us if you are the Messiah, the Son of God." Jesus said to him, "You have said so. But I tell you, from now on you will see the Son of Man seated at the right hand of Power and coming on the clouds of heaven." Then the high priest tore his clothes and said, "He has blasphemed! Why do we still need witnesses? You have now heard his blasphemy. What is your verdict?" They answered, "He deserves death." Then they spat in his face and struck him; and some slapped him, saying, "Prophesy to us, you Messiah! Who is it that struck you?" Peter, who was sitting there to see the end, was asked by a servant girl, "you were with Jesus?" Peter denied it three times and heard a cock crow. Peter remembered Jesus saying, "Before the cock crows, you will deny me three times." And he went out and wept bitterly.

Jesus (PBUH) Before Pilate

Now Jesus stood before the governor, and the governor asked him, "Are you the King of the Jews?" Jesus said, "You say so." But when he was accused by the chief priests and elders, he did not answer. Then Pilate said to him, "Do you not hear how many accusations they make against you?" But he gave him no answer, not even to a single charge, so that the governor was greatly amazed. Now at the festival the governor was accustomed to release a prisoner for the crowd, anyone whom they wanted. At that time they had a notorious prisoner, called Jesus Barabbas. So after they had gathered, Pilate said to them, "Whom do you want me to release for you, Jesus Barabbas or Jesus who is called the Messiah?" For he realised that it was out of jealousy that they had handed him over. The governor again said to them, "Which of the two do you want me to release for you?" And they said, "Barabbas." Pilate said to them, "Then what should I do with Jesus who is called the Messiah?" All of them said, "Let him be crucified!" Then he asked, "Why, what evil has he done?" But they shouted all the more, "Let him be crucified!" So when Pilate saw that he could do nothing, but rather that a riot was beginning, he took some water and washed his hands before the crowd, saying, "I am innocent of this man's blood; see to it yourselves." Then the people as a whole answered, "His blood be on us and on our children!" So he released Barabbas for them; and after flogging Jesus, he handed him over to be crucified. Soldiers, after twisting some thorns into a crown, put it on his head. They put a reed in his right hand and knelt before him and mocked him, saying, "Hail, King of the Jews!" They spat on him, and took the reed and struck him on the head.

Crucifixion
As they went out, they came upon a man from Cyrene named Simon; they compelled this man to carry his cross. Two robbers were also crucified with him, one on the right and one on the left. From noon on, darkness came over the whole land until three in the afternoon. And about three o'clock Jesus cried with a loud voice, "Eli, Eli, lema sabachthani?" that is, "My God, my God, why have you forsaken me?" After this, when Jesus knew that all was now finished, he said (in order to fulfil the scripture), "I am thirsty." A jar full of sour wine was standing there. So they put a sponge full of the wine on a branch of hyssop and held it to

his mouth. When Jesus had received the wine, he said, "It is finished." Then he bowed his head and gave up his spirit. Since it was the day of Preparation, the Jews did not want the bodies left on the cross during the Sabbath, especially because that Sabbath was a day of great solemnity. So they asked Pilate to have the legs of the crucified men broken and the bodies removed. Then the soldiers came and broke the legs of the first and of the other who had been crucified with him. But when they came to Jesus and saw that he was already dead, they did not break his legs. Instead, one of the soldiers pierced his side with a spear, and at once blood and water came. And when they had crucified him, they divided his garments among them by casting lots. At that moment the curtain of the temple was torn in two, from top to bottom. The earth shook, and the rocks were split. Now, when the centurion and those with him who were keeping watch over Jesus, saw the earthquake and what took place, they were terrified and said, "Truly this man was God's Son!"

Jesus (PBUH) is Buried
When it was evening, there came a rich man from Arimathea, named Joseph, who was also a disciple of Jesus. He went to Pilate and asked for the body of Jesus; then Pilate ordered it to be given to him. So Joseph took the body and wrapped it in a clean linen cloth and laid it in his own new tomb, which he had hewn in the rock. He then rolled a great stone to the door of the tomb and went away. Mary Magdalene and the other Mary were there, sitting opposite the tomb. The next day, that is, after the day of Preparation, the chief priests and the Pharisees gathered before Pilate and said, "Sir, we remember what that impostor said while he was still alive, 'After three days I will rise again.' Therefore command the tomb to be made secure

until the third day; otherwise his disciples may go and steal him away, and tell the people, 'He has been raised from the dead,' and the last deception would be worse than the first." Pilate said to them, "You have a guard of soldiers; go, make it as secure as you can." So they went with the guard and made the tomb secure by sealing the stone.

Resurrection

After the Sabbath, as the first day of the week was dawning, Mary Magdalene and the other Mary went to see the tomb. And suddenly there was a great earthquake; for an angel of the Lord, descending from heaven, came and rolled back the stone and sat on it. His appearance was like lightning and his clothing white as snow. For fear of him the guards shook and became like dead men. But the angel said to the women, "Do not be afraid; I know that you are looking for Jesus who was crucified. He is not here; for he has been raised, as he said. Come, see the place where he lay. Then go quickly and tell his disciples, 'He has been raised from the dead, and indeed he is going ahead of you to Galilee; there you will see him.' This is my message for you." Suddenly Jesus met them and said, "Greetings!" And they came to him, took hold of his feet, and worshipped him. Chief priests with elders assembled, they gave a sufficient sum of money to the soldiers and said, "Tell the people, His disciples came by night and stole him away while we were asleep." So they took the money and did as they were directed, and this story has been spread among the Jews to this day.

Now the 11 disciples went to Galilee, to the mountain to which Jesus had directed them. When they saw him, they worshipped him; but some doubted. And Jesus came and said to them, "All authority in heaven and on earth has been given to me. Go therefore and make disciples of all nations, baptizing them in the name of the Father and of the Son and of the Holy Spirit, and teaching them to obey everything that I have commanded you. And remember, I am with you always, to the end of the age."

Second Coming of Jesus (PBUH)

*At that time men will see the Son of Man coming in the clouds with great power and glory. And he will send his angels and gather his elect from the four winds, from the ends of the earth to the ends of the heavens. **(Mark 13:26,27)***

*And I will show portents in the heaven above and signs on the earth below, blood, and fire, and smoky mist. The sun shall be turned to darkness and the moon to blood, before the coming of the Lord's great and glorious day. Then everyone who calls on the name of the Lord shall be saved.' **(Acts 2:19-21)***

*"See, I am coming soon; my reward is with me, to repay according to everyone's work. I am the Alpha and the Omega, the first and the last, the beginning and the end." **(Revelation 22:12,13)***

Teachings of Jesus (PBUH)

Let us read and try to understand the philosophy and psychology of Jesus' teachings given in the Bible. The teachings of Jesus were in parables for the common man, as written in the prophecies. The disciples asked Jesus about the purpose of parables. He said, "To you it has been given to know the secrets of the kingdom of God, but for others they are in parables, so that 'seeing may not see, and hearing they may not understand.'"

Who is Truly Blessed? "Blessed are those who hunger and thirst for righteousness, for they will be filled. Blessed are the merciful, for they will receive mercy. Blessed are the pure in heart, for they will see God. Blessed are the peacemakers, for they will be called children of God." **(Matthew 5:6-9)**

Jesus and the Law. "Do not think that I have come to abolish the law or the prophets; I have come not to abolish but to fulfil. For truly I tell you, until heaven and earth pass away, not one letter, not one stroke of a letter, will pass from the law until all is accomplished." **(Matthew 5:17,18)**

About Anger and Grievance. "But I say to you that if you are angry with a brother or sister, you will be liable to judgement." **(Matthew 5:21,22)**

Love Your Enemies. "But I say to you, Love your enemies and pray for those who persecute you." **(Matthew 5:44)**

About Lust and Adultery. "But I say to you that everyone who looks at a woman with lust has already committed adultery with her in his heart." **(Matthew 5:28)**

About Divorce. "But I say to you that anyone who divorces his wife, except on the ground of unchaste, causes her to commit adultery; and whoever marries a divorced woman commits adultery." **(Matthew 5:31,32)**

Retaliation. "But if anyone strikes you on the right cheek, turn the other also." **(Matthew 5:38-40,42)**

Giving to the Needy "So whenever you give alms, do not sound a trumpet before you, as the hypocrites do in the synagogues and in the streets." **(Matthew 6:2-4)**

Lords Prayers. "And whenever you pray, do not be like the hypocrites. But whenever you pray, go into your room and shut the door and pray to your Father who is in secret; and your Father who sees in secret will reward you." **(Matthew 6:5,6)**

Fasting. "And whenever you fast, do not look dismal, like the hypocrites." **(Matthew 6:16-18)**

Judging Others. "Do not judge, so that you may not be judged. For with the judgement you make you will be judged, and the measure you give will be the measure you get." **(Matthew 7:1-3)**

Golden Rule. "In everything do to others as you would have them do to you; for this is the law and the prophets." **(Matthew 7:12)**

What defiles a Person. "There is nothing outside a person that by going in can defile, but the things that come out are what defile." **(Mark 7:15)**

You will notice that there is a deep-rooted philosophy and psychology behind Jesus' spiritual teachings. It is based upon the love and kindness, peace and tolerance, forgiveness, charity, mercy, and purity of mind, a few to mention to the height of decency of humanity. Jesus' teachings are not for one self, but regards and respect for others, others and others, especially the needy, the suppressed and the victims, to please God. We can also notice Jesus' teachings about the purity of mind, patience, tolerance, helping the needy, peace, prayers and fasting but not a show off, exactly like the messages we find in the Holy Qur'an. I am sure you will agree with me that the central message of Jesus (PBUH) is to, 'be mindful of God and do good deeds,' which is exactly the same central message of the Holy Qur'an.

About Sins

My little children, I am writing these things to you so that you may not sin. But if anyone does sin, we have an advocate with the Father, Jesus Christ the righteous; and he is the atoning sacrifice for our sins, and not for ours only but also for the sins of the whole world. **(1 John 2:1,2)**

Some of the Disputed Prophecies Between the Jews, Christians and Muslims

About Elijah/John the Baptist

A voice cries out: "In the wilderness prepare the way of the Lord, make straight in the desert a highway for our God." **(Isaiah 40:3)**

Lo, I will send you the Prophet Elijah before the great and terrible day of the Lord comes. **(Malachi 4:5)**

There is a difference of opinion about the above prophecies between the Jews, the Christians and the Muslims. Jewish priests and Levites went from Jerusalem to ask Jesus, where is Elijah who would come in his second coming before the Messiah (Malachi 4:5)? Also as per the prophecy, the Jews were expecting a prophet. When they asked Jesus, where is Elijah? he said, "John the Baptist." When they went to confirm from John the Baptist, who was in prison, he confirmed that he was neither the Messiah, nor Elijah, nor that prophet, and He said, "I am the voice of one crying in the wilderness, make straight the way of the Lord, as the Prophet Isaiah said" (John 1:19-23). Jesus later on replied to the question of his disciples that Elijah has already come and they did not recognise him, but they did to him whatever they pleased. So also the son of man is about to suffer at their hands (Matthew 17:10-12). The disciples then understood that Jesus was referring to John the Baptist performing the role of Elijah. Jews rejected Jesus after John the Baptist's confirmation that he was neither the Messiah, nor Elijah, nor that prophet. The Christians believe that John the Baptist confirmed that he was the voice crying out in the wilderness, make straight the way for the Lord, as the Prophet Isaiah said, so John the Baptist was performing the role of Elijah. Every word that Jesus said was the word of God, and if Jesus himself said that John the Baptist was Elijah, than Jesus' word is final and a true spiritual interpretation as per the Christians. As regards the Jews also asking John the Baptist, "Are you that Prophet?" the Muslims believe that, this question was about the coming of Prophet Muhammad as per the prophecies in the Holy Bible like: Genesis 21:12,13,18,19,21, 25:13. Deut 33:1,2. Isaiah, 29:11,12, 42:11.

A New Prophet Like Moses [(PBUH)]

'The Lord God will raise up a prophet like me (Moses) from among your own people' (Deut 18:15). The Christians believe that Jesus was like Moses (Acts 3:22), whereas the Muslims believe Muhammad was like Moses. Most Bibles say, a prophet like Moses among your brothers. The similarities about Moses if compared, about the birth, marriage, children, natural death or raised alive, the second

41

coming, God incarnate or man like Moses, it is fair to say that it is like Muhammad. Abraham had two sons, Isaac and Ishmael, and their children are cousin brothers. Jesus and Muhammad both are among their brothers. (PBUT)

Miracles of Jesus (PBUH)
The miracles of Jesus started even before his miraculous birth from his mother Mary who conceived Jesus as a virgin without any male intervention. Jesus gave life to the dead and eyesight to the born blind and leper, and cured the needy. However the first miracle during his life given in the Gospels is about making water into wine at a wedding party at Cana in Galilee as per John Chapter 2:1-11, whereas the first miracle of his life in the Qur'an is that, he spoke as an infant to defend his mother as per the Qur'an 19:27-34, see under the heading 'Jesus and Mary in the Qur'an.'

There were many other miracles, giving life to the dead, healed the born blind and leper, taking out the evil spirits, walked on the water, foretold about his departure from this world that, 'the hour is coming,' foretold that one of his disciples will betray him, foretold Peter will deny him three times before the cock crows, are only a few to mention. The Qur'an also confirms that Jesus (PBUH) gave life to the dead, cured the born blind and leper, with God's permission.

Jesus (PBUH) for Jews Only?
Jesus was born into a Jewish family and he started his message about the laws of Moses and was teaching to Jews only, however his teachings was not bound literally to the letters like Jews, but the spirit of the letters, because the Jews' Rabbis were suppressing the people, the way they were using the law of Moses. There are prophecies about Jesus (PBUH) in Isaiah and Psalms (mentioned above) which

declared that his own people will reject him, while gentile (non Jews) will believe him. During his lifetime Jesus ⁽ᴾᴮᵁᴴ⁾ focused his teachings only to the Jews (Matthew 10:5-7, 15:22-24), till the fulfilment of all the prophecies up to his resurrection to proclaim to the gentiles. Therefore after his resurrection, Jesus said to his disciples, "All authority in heaven and on earth has been given to me. Go therefore and make disciples of all nations baptising them in the name of the Father and of the Son and of the Holy Spirit, teaching them to observe all that I have commanded you. And behold, I am with you always, to the end of the age" (Matthew 28:18-20).

Apostles therefore went to the rest of the world preaching about the fulfilment of the prophecies about Jesus,⁽ᴾᴮᵁᴴ⁾ which was appropriate only after the resurrection, and they also performed miracles in the name of Jesus.⁽ᴾᴮᵁᴴ⁾

The Muslims' understanding from the Bible and the Qur'an is that during his lifetime, Jesus proclaimed and instructed his disciples not to go to gentiles (non Jews), but to the Jews only. Muslims do not believe in the resurrection of Jesus, as revealed in the Holy Qur'an, Jesus ⁽ᴾᴮᵁᴴ⁾ was raised up by God to Himself, and that he did not die on the Cross (Qur'an 3:49, 4:197).

Jesus ⁽ᴾᴮᵁᴴ⁾ Son of God?

For God so loved the world that he gave his only Son, so that everyone who believes in him may not perish but may have eternal life. *(John 3:16)*

There are sons by tons in the Bible, a few as an example like, Exodus 4:22,23, Luke 3:38, Romans 8:14, Matthew 5:9, which in the Biblical language means Godly person. However, the Christians say Jesus is the only, 'begotten son of God,' which has been translated from the Greek word Monogenes which means, 'the only one of its kind', which was the fulfilment of the prophecy.

The Qur'an also confirms the miraculous birth of Jesus from virgin Mary, a word of truth about which the people are in doubt (Qur'an 19:34-36). However, the Qur'an denies Jesus the son of God, and that Jesus ^(PBUH) was a Messenger and a man like other prophets.

Did Jesus ^(PBUH) Claim Divinity?

The Christians believe that God visited our earth in the form of Jesus as per the fulfilment of the prophecies in the Old Testament of the Bible. They believe in one God, but worship trinity (God the Father, the Son and the Holy Spirit) as three characteristics of one and the same God.
As per the understanding of the Muslims, there is not a single unequivocal statement in the whole Bible where Jesus himself claimed divinity or he himself said that I am God and worship me. The Muslims' understanding from the statements of Jesus in the Bible, such as, "Hear, O Israel: the Lord our God, the Lord is one" (Mark 12:28,29), "I have come not to abolish but to fulfil the law" (Matthew 5:17,18), "The Father and I are one (one in purpose)" (John 10:30), "I can do nothing at my own" (John 8:28), "a man attested to you by God" (John 14:1,2), are repeated messages where Jesus did not claim divinity, instead he was denying it. Also is revealed in the Qur'an that 'Jesus did not claim divinity, he was a man and a prophet, strengthened with the Holy Spirit.'

The Christian belief about the above referred texts about Jesus are different to the Muslims' understanding.

44

According to the Christians, Jesus (PBUH) was making it clear to them that the Lord is one, and he is not a separate entity, "I and my Father are one." And about the unprecedented miracles, he was telling that it is not possible for any human including him in his human form to perform such miracles, but with the will of his Father in heaven, which are the characteristics of the one and the same God.

Crucifixion
The details of the crucifixion of Jesus (PBUH) as per the belief of the Christians have been explained earlier. There is another version that, instead of Jesus, it was another person who happened to be on the Cross. The Qur'an 4:157 reveals that, 'they neither killed him, nor crucified him, **it was made to appear like that to them.** God raised him up to Himself.' During an interfaith dialogue with some Christians, they said that we both are right according to your Holy Qur'an. The people around that time believed what was made to appear like that to them, and you are right to believe what was revealed to you 600 years after Jesus. The people did not witness Jesus (PBUH) being raised by God to Himself at the time of Crucifixion, but they did witness Jesus being raised by God to Himself after the resurrection, and that it was a prophecy fulfilled. In reply, I said Jesus (PBUH) must have been replaced by another man on the Cross, and raised by God to Himself at the will of God. Details are given under the heading, 'A Trial to Proclaim to the Christians.'

Resurrection
Besides the prophecies about the resurrection mentioned above, Jesus (PBUH) himself gave a sign about resurrection as below, which is usually disputed.

The Sign of Jonah

Jonah was a prophet before Jesus, and there was a very famous miracle about him. In brief, Jonah was commanded by God to go to a town of Nineveh (Assyria) to proclaim, which he ignored. While he was travelling on a ship to Tarshish, it got caught up in a heavy sea storm. According to the custom of the Jews, they cast lots to find the sinner, which fell to Jonah. He was thrown in the sea and the whale swallowed him and he prayed to God while he was in its belly. After three days and three nights, the whale spat Jonah on the sea shore and he was alive all this time praying to God. Some of the doctors of the law and the Pharisees said, "Master, we like you to show us a sign," and he replied.

For just as Jonah was three days and three nights in the belly of the sea monster, so for three days and three nights the Son of Man will be in the heart of the earth. **(Matthew 12:40)**

The sign given by Jesus about the miracle of Jonah, 'Like Jonah was three days and three nights in the belly of whale' is the most significant reference to Jesus' crucifixion and resurrection. If it is compared to Jesus on the Cross on Friday afternoon and Sunday morning, his body as per the Christians, was missing, or as per Jews was stolen by his disciples. The sign about Jonah does not cover the period of three days and three nights in the heart of the earth. Also that Jonah was alive all the time in the belly of the whale praying to God, as against the belief that Jesus died on the cross. However one of the various responses from the Christians is that the Jews' way of describing day and night at the time was different to what we have today, and it was exactly three days and three nights according to their understanding of that time as below:

That the Son of Man must be handed over to sinners, and be crucified, and on the third day rise again. (Luke 24:7)

Like Jonah was delivered into the mammal, Jesus was also delivered into the hands of sinful men on Thursday evening (half day), crucified and buried on Friday, and raised from the dead on Sunday morning (half day), which comes to three days and three nights.

The Christians believe in the Crucifixion of Jesus, that he died for the sins of many and was resurrected as below:

Isaiah 53:4-5. One who would die for the sins of many. Fulfilled (1 Corinthian 15:17, and Gospels).

John 2:19,21. Jesus foretold about his death.

Crucifixion and the burial of the body was witnessed by many.

Mark 15:46 and Luke 23:53. Body was laid in the Tomb.

The body in the Tomb was guarded by the soldiers. The punishment for a Roman guard falling asleep was death.

Over 500 people (eye witnesses) saw Jesus' resurrected body.

The disciples who believed in the fulfilment of the prophecy, started to preach Jesus' message, taking risk of torture, persecution and death.

The Apostles performed the miracles in the name of Jesus to cure those in need, which is evidence of truth about Jesus' resurrection.

Also about resurrection. Acts 2:23-36, 13:23-37.

In the Qur'an, the divinity, trinity, crucifixion, resurrection, and Jesus being son of God is denied (Qur'an 4:157,158,171, 5:73,75).

The second coming of Jesus (PBUH). The Qur'an confirms the second coming of Jesus.

'Surely Jesus is a sign of the Hour' ***(Qur'an 43:61)***.

'There is not any one of the People of Book who will not believe in Jesus before his death, and on the Day of Resurrection he will be a witness against them' ***(Qur'an 4:159)***.

Notes

The faith of Christianity has always sparked passionate and diverse opinions about Christ's death on the Cross and resurrection, which are the very foundation of their faith. Christians believe that, on a quiet Sunday morning three days after Jesus was crucified, the worlds greatest miracle took place, when Jesus rose from the dead, which is believed to be the fulfilment of the prophecy through Jesus. Gospel of Matthew, Mark, Luke and John explain about the resurrection of Jesus, but they differ about the details of that morning about the number of women and the angels who witnessed.

The doctrine of Christianity has been influenced the most by Paul, a Jew by birth (Saul), speaker of Greek, a citizen of Rome, a persecutor of the Christians, and later an Apostle of the Christians (Paul) who was beheaded by Romans for preaching Christianity. Paul preached that, Christ has redeemed us from the curse of the law and what matters is, the spirit of faith in Christ. **(Galatians 3:23-29)**

About Islam

Let us now see why we Muslims believe what we believe! About Muhammad! The Qur'an! Different factions! The purpose of life of the Muslims! Relationship of Muslims with the People of Book! Our Nearest Friends are Christians, Reveals the Qur'an! Proclaim! **Four Step Guide!**

About Muhammad (PBUH)

The prophecies about the coming of Muhammad (PBUH) were given in the New Testament and Old Testament of the Bible, hundreds of years before the birth of Muhammad (see under the prophecies about Muhammad). Before proceeding to the life of Muhammad (PBUH), it is important to know briefly about the people of Mecca and the different tribes of the desert of Arabia. The religion of most people in Mecca and Arabia at the beginning of Muhammad's lifetime was polytheism, though Christianity and Judaism were also practised in some areas. Most of the people worshipped idols, the sun and the moon, and also a chief god. It was a tribal system, and various tribes used to continuously fight each other for power. There was no central government and the tribal chiefs of each tribe had all the power and control and were exploiting the common man to their advantage, particularly women, children and the poor. Mecca was a centre for religion and trade. Ka'ba was built by Abraham and his son Ishmael in Mecca to worship one God, but was corrupted by the idol worshippers who were in the majority. Mecca was also a famous trade route to Yemen during the winters and to Syria during the summers.

Muhammad $^{(PBUH)}$ was born in Mecca about the year 570 AD and his father Abdullah had died before he was born. His mother Amina also died when he was six years of age, and he became an orphan a second time. As an orphan child he was taken care of by his grandfather, Abdul Mutlib, who also died two years later, when he was eight years of age, and he became an orphan a third time. His uncle Abu Talib started to look after him, who was a poor man, and Muhammad started to work as a Shepherd to earn and contribute to the large family of his uncle. While he was in his twenties, he was employed by a rich and highly respected lady Khudija. During the period when he was working for Khudija, she was so impressed with his honesty, distinguished character, and nobality in his personality that she proposed marriage to him. He married when he was twenty five years of age and Khudija was forty years old. They were married for over 25 years, till Khudija died when he was 49 years old and a prophet, living in Mecca.

Muhammad $^{(PBUH)}$ was always disturbed by the injustices and exploitation of the weak and poor of society. When he was at the age of 40 he received the first revelation of the Qur'an in the cave of Hira near Mecca, and started his mission as a prophet. Even before he started his mission as a prophet, he was highly respected as a peacemaker. The preaching of the Qur'an was mainly focused upon the equality and justice, which was against the prevailing social order and was a direct threat to the power of the Chiefs of all the tribes, who condemned Muhammad and his message. While his followers grew in numbers, the opposition grew stronger as well. The opposition from other tribes of Mecca, though, was growing bitter, but they could not dare to openly challenge Muhammad into a direct clash, due to the fear of his uncle Abu Talib who was the Chief of the powerful

Hashim tribe. His uncle, though, was his guardian from a young age, who never accepted Islam during his life, but he made sure to protect his nephew, Muhammad (PBUH), from the opposing tribes. Although Abu Talib did not embrace Islam, Muhammad had all the love and respect for him. At the same time his other uncle, Abu Lahab was extremely jealous of his popularity and became his strong enemy, quite openly. Things went from bad to worse when his wife Khudija and his uncle Abu Talib died in the same year, which was a big setback for him, and this year became known as the year of grief.

Soon after, the Prophet (PBUH) experienced a Night Journey and Ascension to Heaven. He was accompanied by the angel Gabriel from Mecca to Jerusalem and then to Heaven. While the followers in Mecca were growing fast in numbers, the tribes from Yathrib (Medina) who were also influenced by his fair judgement as a peacemaker in Mecca and his teachings, accepted his faith. Different tribes of Medina were at each other's throat and they needed a peacemaker to whom they all could trust and it was Muhammad. They were also aware of the persecution of the Muslims from Meccans, therefore they invited him and his followers to seek sanctuary in Yathrib. The migration of Muslims to Medina took place during the year 622 AD, and is known as Hijra, which has been adopted as the start of the Muslim calendar.

Soon after arrival in Yathrib, Muhammad (PBUH) built the first mosque of Islam, where he preached the message of the Qur'an and changed the attitudes of different communities into a brotherhood, and established mutual respect for each other. The different tribes respected him like a father figure, and the religion Islam started to spread in Yathrib at such a fast pace, that Yathrib became known as Medinat al-Nabi (the City of the Prophet) or Medina. He made pacts with other tribes giving them equal rights and freedom to practice their religions, and will defend their city in case of an attack. At this stage, the Muslims had their own state, and how to govern the Muslim state, the revelations began containing legislation on all aspects of life for Muslims, and how to defend their states. A number of battles took place, starting with the Battle of Badr during 624 AD, where Muslims defeated the much larger Meccan Army. It was followed by Battle of Uhud during 625 AD, where Muslims were defeated by the Meccan Army. The Battle of Trench took place during 627 AD, where the Meccan Army attacked Medina, but failed to capture it. They suffered heavy casualties and withdrew. During AH6, the Meccans denied the Muslims to undertake a pilgrimage to Mecca. The negotiations took place and a truce agreement for 10 years, known as 'Sulah Hudaybiyya' was accepted by Muslims. According to the truce agreement, the Muslims returned to Medina without performing the pilgrimage and planned to return the next year to finish it. However, during AH8, one of the Meccan allies broke the truce agreement and there was no other option for Muslims but either to surrender or to fight to practice their religion. The Muslims gave an ultimatum of war, and after the deadline was over they advanced to attack Mecca. The common man in Mecca and the surrounding areas by now were in favour of the religion of Muhammad, and the Meccan leaders had lost the support of their people who were the victims of their suppression for generations. The tribal leaders being in a helpless situation, decided to surrender without fighting and embraced Islam. The Prophet gave a general amnesty to all, including his staunch enemies, and vowed to protect each person's life, property and dignity, regardless of race, religion, colour and gender.

The desert tribe people all over the Arabian Peninsula were so impressed with the Prophet's generosity of general amnesty for all, that they started to embrace Islam, one after the other. In AH10, the Prophet, during his last pilgrimage to Mecca, gave a famous farewell speech on the Mount of Mercy. The theme of his speech was the righteous deeds, equality of human rights and dignity, peace and justice. Soon after his final farewell speech in year 632 AD, he returned to Medina, and shortly thereafter he died. By this time, the whole of the Arabian Peninsula had accepted Islam and united under the banner of Islam, as one Muslim state. The most beautiful guideline for Muslims is the last Sermon of Prophet Muhammad (PBUH). After praising and thanking God (in brief below), he said:

*"Hurt no one so that no one may hurt you. Remember you will indeed meet your Lord, and that **He will indeed reckon your deeds.** All mankind are from Adam and Eve, a white has no superiority over a black, nor a black has any superiority over white, except by **piety and good deeds."***

The Qur'an reveals that the Prophet Muhammad (PBUH) was the seal of the prophets and the Messenger of God.

Muhammad is not the father of any of your men, but he is the Messenger of God and the seal of the prophets.
(Qur'an 33:40)

There are no suitable words to express his true personality, but a few words in his honour to say that,

Muhammad (PBUH) was a three time orphan child (including a born orphan), a shepherd, a peacemaker, a prophet, a messenger, a teacher, a judge, an arbitrator, a consoler, a legislator, a philosopher, an orator, a warrior, a conqueror

of ideas, a father figure, and a seal of the prophets. As per many renowned non Muslim writers, 'the greatest man that ever lived in our world was Muhammad' (PBUH).

Prophecies about the Coming of Muhammad (PBUH)

For though Isaac shall your offspring be named. And I will make a nation of the son of the slave woman also, because he is your offspring. (Genesis 21:12,13)

These are the names of the sons of Ishmael, named in the order of their birth: Nebaioth, the firstborn of Ishmael; and Kedar, Adbeel, Mibsam. (Genesis 25:13)

This is a very important prophecy in the Holy Bible, that God made a covenant with Abraham, to raise prophets from his offspring. Muhammad (PBUH) was also the offspring from Kedar, Ishmael and Abraham.

The Lord your God will raise up for you a prophet like me from among your own people; you shall heed such a prophet. (Deut 18:15)

Moses said, "The Lord your God will raise up for you from your own people a prophet like me. You must listen to whatever he tells you." (Acts 3:22)

A New Prophet like Moses (PBUH). Based upon the above prophecies Christians believe that Jesus was like Moses, whereas The Muslims believe Muhammad was like Moses. Most Bibles say, a prophet like Moses among your brothers. The similarities about Moses if compared,' the birth, marriage, children, natural death or raised alive, the second coming, and God incarnate or man like Moses', it is fair to say that it is like Muhammad. Abraham had two sons Isaac and Ishmael, and their children are cousin brothers. Both Jesus and Muhammad are among brothers [PBUT].

The vision of all this has become for you like the words of a sealed document. If it is given to those who can read, with the command, "Read this," they say, "We cannot, for it is sealed." And if it is given to those who cannot read, saying, "Read this," they say, "We cannot read." **(Isaiah 29:11,12)**

Read! In the name of your Lord who created all. **(Qur'an 96:1)**

It was a well known fact among the close family and the tribes of Prophet Muhammad [PBUH] in Medina that he was an illiterate person who could not read and write. As per the above prophecy, the first time when Angel Gabriel asked Muhammad to read, he replied, "I cannot read." This itself was a sign of a miracle for the people around who knew him from his childhood, and also the fulfilment of the prophecy. After he started to receive the revelations, he was teaching others, while he could not read and write himself.

"Come, lift up the boy and hold him fast with your hand, for I will make a great nation of him." Then God opened her eyes and she saw a well of water. She went, and filled the skin with water, and gave the boy a drink. He lived in the wilderness of Paran; and his mother got a wife for him from the land of Egypt. **(Genesis 21:18,19,21)**

This is a significant incident in the history of Muslims, where the wife of Abraham, Hager, with her small son Ishmael, crying thirsty of water, was running in between two hills in search of water. God heard their cry, and made spring water gush from a well known as Zamzam. In remembrance of this event, Muslims run between two hills of Al-Safa and Al-Marwa during their pilgrimage of Haj. Ishmael lived in Paran (Mecca), and God fulfilled His promise by raising Prophet Muhammad who was his descendent.

"The oracle concerning the desert plain. In the scrub of the desert plain you will lodge, O caravans of Dedanites. Bring water to the thirsty, meet the fugitive with bread, O inhabitants of the land of Tema. For they have fled from the swords, from the drawn sword, from the bent bow, and from the stress of battle. For thus the Lord said to me: Within a year, according to the years of a hired worker, all the glory of Kedar will come to an end; and the remaining bows of Kedar's warriors will be few; for the Lord, the God of Israel, has spoken." **(Isaiah 21:13-17)**

The above prophecy is about the first Battle of Badr, between the children of Ishmael, the children of Tema settled in Medina, and the children of Kedar settled in Mecca. A small number of Muslims (313) of Medina defeated a large number of the Meccan Army of over 1,000.

"I still have many things to say to you, but you cannot bear them now. When the Spirit of truth comes, he will guide you into all the truth; for he will not speak on his own, but will speak whatever he hears, and he will declare to you the things that are to come. He will glorify me, because he will take what is mine and declare it to you. All that the Father has is mine. For this reason I said that he will take what is mine and declare it to you." **(John 16:12-15)**

"I have said these things to you while I am still with you. But the Advocate, the Holy Spirit, whom the Father will send in my name, will teach you everything, and remind you of all that I have said to you." **(John 14:25,26)**

"Nevertheless I tell you the truth: it is to your advantage that I go away, for if I do not go away, the Advocate will not come to you; but if I go, I will send him to you." **(John 16:7)**

Note. Muslims believe that the name Ahmad [(PBUH)] is used in original script, the English translation reads as helper, comforter, advocate.

"And I will ask the Father, and he will give you another Advocate, to be with you forever. This is the Spirit of truth, whom the world cannot receive, because it neither sees him nor knows him. You know him, because he abides with you, and he will be in you." **(John 14:16,17)**

Note. There are differences about the translation of initial Hebrew language of the phrase ending, 'for ever' or 'in time.' Most scholars are in favour of in time. There is also difference on Helper being the Holy Spirit or Spirit of Truth. Some verses refer to Helper as Holy Spirit, while other verses refer to it as the Spirit of Truth. Christians believe it as the Holy Spirit, while Muslims believe, the Spirit of Truth refers to the messenger Prophet Muhammad [(PBUH)].

Happy are those who live in your house, ever singing your praise. (Selah) Happy are those whose strength is in you, in whose heart are the highways to Zion. As they go through the valley of Baca they make it a place of springs; the early rain also covers it with pools. **(Psalms 84:4-6)**

Note. Mecca was known as Baca, where Muhammad (PBUH) was born and lived with his family and tribe.

In addition to the prophecies in the Old Testament and New Testament of the Bible, there are also several prophecies about the coming of Muhammad (PBUH) in Hindu scriptures about his name, birth place, date of birth, his father and mother's names, his qualities, battles with results, will guide to truth and as a last and final prophet who will be revealed the eternal law. Of all the prophecies, the most important is the very first one mentioned above (Genesis 21:12,13), which is the foundation of the faith of the religions of Judaism, Christianity and Islam. The other prophecies, even if they remain disputed, there can be no dispute on this prophecy between the Jews, Christians and the Muslims, as it is recorded in their Bible. God simply fulfilled His promise by raising Muhammad (PBUH) as a prophet and a messenger to whom the Qur'an was revealed.

The Holy Qur'an

Every word of the Holy Qur'an is a word of God, is the belief of the Muslims. The words of Prophet Muhammad and the stories by the historians are recorded separately. The Qur'an is the supreme authority in Islam, and the life of the Muslims is built around the Qur'an. It is the fundamental source of the creed, rituals, and laws of the Islamic religion and differentiates between right and wrong. It is a source of guidance on all the aspects of the life of Muslims. It confirms the same faith of Abraham, islam (complete submission/devotion to God), and a law and path for the Muslims to follow with the ultimate objective to, 'be mindful of God and do good deeds.' When Angel Gabriel approached Muhammad (PBUH), and asked him to read in the name of the

Lord, he replied that he could not read. The angel recited to him the first two lines of the Qur'an 96:1-5, which began the Qur'an and the mission of the Prophet Muhammad (PBUH). The prophecy of Muhammad (PBUH) who could not read and write is also given in the Bible, Isaiah 29 (11,12) as mentioned above. The Prophet always recited the revelations to the Scribes and other people around him, and ensured that it was recorded as revealed and instructed by Gabriel. The Qur'an was revealed step by step over a period of 23 years, completed and recorded during the life of the Prophet. The people around the Prophet were well aware of the fact that he could not read and write. This itself was a miracle for them and they believed in him whole-heartedly. During the second year after the Prophet's death, 633 AD, the successor to the Prophet and first Caliph, Abu Bakar, arranged a written copy of the complete Qur'an and kept it safe with him. It was during the time of the third Caliph Uthman, when the Islamic state had expanded vastly, that the Caliph arranged to make copies from the original Qur'an and distributed them to the different parts of the Muslim world. This is the Qur'an, recorded and preserved word by word, as revealed about 1400 years ago, which is to be read and understood, as a source of guidance from God for the whole of humanity. The Qur'an reveals the laws to govern the Muslim community with regard to marriage, commerce and finance, relations with other communities, war and peace. The Qur'an contains 114 Suras consisting of some 6200 verses, to include the rituals of worship, personal laws, civil laws, penal laws, and judiciary matters and testimony, with general principles rather than detailed laws. A verse may contain several sentences, and a sentence on its own can be used on its own, which can be misinterpreted, and is usually exploited by non-Muslims to criticise Islam and also by some Misguided Muslims.

The Holy Qur'an reveals that, this Book is a clear explanation of everything in various ways, so that you may understand (Qur'an 6:65,114,16:89). A Muslim should live by the examples (Sunnah) of Prophet Muhammad (PBUH).

The Holy Qur'an and Modern Science

Albert Einstein famously said that, "Science without religion is Lame, and Religion without science is Blind." There are so many signs (versus) in the Qur'an which lead science to a direction to prove it to be surely true. A few of the signs, among others, which have been confirmed by science to be true are mentioned below.

Big bang theory. 30 to 40 years back, a group of scientists confirmed that initially the whole universe was one primary Nebula, then there was a secondary separation, a big bang. Galaxies, stars, the sun and the earth on which we live came in to existence as a result of this big bang. The Qur'an revealed this about 1400 years ago (Qur'an 21:30).

Shape of the earth. Initially it was believed that the earth is flat, later spherical and then go-spherical shape. It was in 1577 that Sir Francis Drake sailed around the earth and proved that the earth is a spherical shape. It was revealed that the earth is of the shape of an Ostrich egg, which is of go-spherical shape. (Qur'an 79:30)

Sun. Initially it was believed that the sun was stationary. It was followed by the belief that the sun revolved, but did not rotate on its own axis. Science has now discovered that the sun, besides revolving, even rotates about its own axis. It was revealed that the sun rotates on its own axis. (Qur'an 21:33, and 36:40)

60

Moon. Initially it was believed that the moon had its own light. It was revealed that while the sun had its own light, the moon had a borrowed/reflected light from the sun. (Qur'an 25:61)

Universe expanding. Until recently, the scientists could not establish as to why the light of the stars is diminishing progressively. It has now been confirmed by the scientists that it is the galaxy that is moving away towards a particular destination in a particular time. It was revealed that God made the universe expand to a vast extent. (Qur'an 51:47)

Atom. Before it was believed by the scientists that the atom is the smallest particle, the Qur'an 10:61 and 34:3 revealed it to be 'smaller or greater than a speck of dust.'

Everything is made in pairs (Qur'an 51:49).

Living creatures are made from water (Qur'an 21:30, 24:45 and 25:54).

Water cycle. The water cycle has been revealed in the Qur'an 15:22, 30:24, 36:34 and also in many more verses.

Mountains are to provide stability and stop the earth from shaking. (Qur'an 16:15, 21:31, 78:6,7, and 79:32).

Embryology. The Qur'an 22:5 and 23:12-14 revealed the different stages of the child in the mother's womb. Qur'an 53:45,46 also revealed the sex of the child depends upon the father's sperm.

Oceanology. The Qur'an 25:53 revealed about two bodies of flowing water, one sweet and one bitter, having unseen barriers.

Finger prints. In 1880, Sir Frances Gold discovered the finger printing method that no two finger prints even in millions of people are identical. The Qur'an 75:3-4 revealed about finger prints.

Today is the age of science and technology. The Qur'an on its own merits is a miracle of miracles for all time to come.

Note. Regardless of belief in the Qur'an, it is beneficial for all the people to understand this Holy Book to seek the directions to explore our world, our universe and much more, in the interest of the whole of humanity. For the Muslims, science or no science, the Qur'an is everything for them, they believe in it whole-heartedly and render unquestioning obedience to God's commandments, and that is how they are supposed to live their life with due regards and kindness for the whole of humanity.

The Real Essence of the Holy Qur'an

The most essential requirement for the Muslims is to understand 'the real essence of the Qur'an.' Islam is a spiritual religion which purifies the soul of a person to achieve God's consciousness to do the righteous deeds. There are repeated revelations in the Qur'an to draw our attention to the ultimate objective to, '**be mindful of God and do good deeds**,' which brings the blessings of God for this life and the life hereafter, as well as protect us from the anger of God and His punishment, due to our wrong doings. The core message in the Qur'an is about Tawheed (unity), which means, the unity of God, unity of His names and attributes and the unity of worship. One third of the Holy Qur'an is about the People of Book (Jews and Christians), and we must know the relationship between the Holy Scriptures and their followers. Let us first see how the religions of the revealed books are prescribed in the Qur'an.

Religion. There are two aspects of the religions of the Jews, Christians and Muslims prescribed in the Qur'an, 'The Faith, and, the Law and Path.' Though these two aspects are interdependent, but as a matter of easy understanding, I will explain it to cover the period before the revealed Holy Books, as well as the time when the Qur'an was revealed.

The Faith

Say (O Muslims), "We believe in God and in what has been sent down to us, and which was sent down to Abraham, Ishmael, Isaac, Jacob, and their offspring, and what has been given to Moses, Jesus and the prophets from their Lord. We make no distinction between any of them. In the matter of faith, we have surrendered to God." (Qur'an 3:84)

In the matters of faith, He has decreed for you the same commandment that He gave Noah, which We have revealed to you and which We enjoined on Abraham and Moses and Jesus: Establish this faith and do not divide into factions within it. (Qur'an 42:13)

'believe in one God, associate no partners with Him and worship none but Him alone'. (Qur'an 3:64)

Complete submission/devotion to God is the faith. The same faith was revealed by God to the people through all the previous prophets, before the Holy Books were revealed, and it has been confirmed to be the same in all the revealed Books. The Qur'an refers the faith by the Arabic word islam (complete submission/devotion to God), as well as the Islam religion (faith combined with law and path).

The law and path

We have prescribed a law and path to each of you. If God had so willed, He would have made you all one community, but He desired to test you in different ways through which He has given to you. So, 'race to do good'. You will all return to God and He will make clear to you the matters you used to dispute about. **(Qur'an 5:48)**

The religions of the Jews, Christians and the Muslims consist of the faith combined with the respective law and path. It is the integral part of the Muslims' religion that with the same faith (complete submission/devotion to God), believe in the Holy Qur'an, believe and obey the Messenger Prophet Muhammad [PBUH], believe in the Last Day, believe in all the previous Scriptures and the prophets. According to the Holy Qur'an, each community has been prescribed a different law and path Qur'an 5:43-48, with a common faith. I will refrain from comparing the different law and path of the Jews, Christians and Muslims, since it is the revelation of God, who is all wise and has prescribed a solution to the problems of each community as He desired. However the ultimate objective revealed for each community is the same to, 'be mindful of God and do good deeds.' Like the law and path revealed in the Torah for the Jews, the Gospels for the Christians, the Qur'an has revealed the law and path for the Muslims which includes, how to govern the Muslim community with legislation, the rituals of worship, the relationship with other communities, right of self defence and other guidelines about the way of life for the Muslims. The details are covered under the heading, 'Relationship of the Muslim Community with the People of Book.'

God has strictly forbidden Muslims to divide in to factions, which is the most serious offence in Islam, as revealed in the Holy Qur'an. However, those who have divided into factions, because they are seeking guidance from the Holy Qur'an as they understand, it has also been revealed that their case rests with God, and He will make clear to them about their differences, when they all return to God, and that they will be rewarded for their righteous deeds.

The Purpose of our Life. The five pillars of Islam revealed in the Holy Qur'an are the most spiritual means to worship God to purify our souls, ask for help and to achieve the ultimate objective and purpose of our life, **'God's consciousness to do good deeds.'** Following are the guidelines in the Qur'an about the purpose of our life.

'I created jinn and humankind only to worship me'. ***(Qur'an 51:56)***

*O people, **It is you who need me.** God alone is self sufficient and All Praiseworthy.* ***(Qur'an 35:15)***

*It is He who has created death and life to test which of you is **excellent in deeds.** **(Qur'an 67:2)***

*Do people think that they will be left alone on mere saying, **"We believe" and will not be tested.** Do the evildoers think they can escape Us?* ***(Qur'an 29:2,4)***

'Do those who commit evil deeds think that We will deal with them in the same way as those who believe and do good deeds, that they will be equal in their life and their death? How ill do they judge. God created the heavens and the earth for a true purpose: to reward each soul

according to its deeds, and they will not be wronged'.
(Qur'an 45:21,22)

So woe to those who worship but are heedless of their prayers; Those who make show of prayers, and lack common kindness. ***(Qur'an 107:4-7)***

The above mentioned verses and also, Qur'an 2:177, 5:9,93, 6:48, 16:12, 19:96, 29:9,57,58, 38:24,49:13 and 99:6-8, are a few of the repeated revelations in the Qur'an to be mindful of God and do good deeds, which is the purpose of our life, and God has promised forgiveness and rich rewards in this world and the world hereafter for the righteous deeds. Being mindful of God means to love God Almighty, as well as fear God from His anger due to our wrong deeds. To worship God does not benefit but pleases God, mainly for our benefit to live in peace and harmony. The Muslims have been commanded that, 'do not think that you believe and will not be tested for your righteous deeds.' If someone offers regular prayers in the mosque, but leads a life with evil deeds, it means that, 'he is not mindful of God, he neither loves nor fears God, it is a deceptive appearance, 'façade'. God knows our intentions and will judge us by our deeds. We may not know others' intentions, but we must judge others by their deeds and not only by their duty of prayers. As regards the prayers, the oppressors, oppressed, evildoers, as well as God fearing people with good deeds, offer prayers in the same church or mosque, which raises a serious question about the prayers of the oppressors and evil doers. The prayers are therefore neither the deeds nor the objective in itself, but the spiritual means to achieve the objective of God's consciousness, which must lead to the righteous deeds, otherwise it is a deceptive appearance, 'façade'. Righteous deeds are therefore a yard stick to measure that a person is mindful of God or otherwise. Indeed the good deeds being mindful of God are the essence of worship, the purpose of our life, and the real essence of the Holy Qur'an.

The end product result for a community focussed upon the essence of the Holy Qur'an, being mindful of God with a culture of righteous deeds will be that, the powerful will not rule but serve the people, establish peace and justice for all, particularly for the minorities, and protect the animals and the environment, which will please God. The best demonstration of culture of righteous deeds was the time of Prophet Muhammad [PBUH] and the rightly guided Caliphs. As against the culture of righteous deeds, the culture of façade (show off) will produce evil doers in control of the affairs of a community or state which will lead to injustice, corruption, discrimination, exploitation, and discrimination against the minorities, cruelty to animals and abuse of the environment, whereas the God fearing people become helpless and victims at the mercy of such a system, which will displease God. In view of the guidelines of the Holy Qur'an, the yard stick to measure a state with the culture of righteous deeds can be based upon the criteria of three basic essentials that a state must provide to her people to please God. Protection (person, property and dignity), Opportunities, and Justice for all. I leave it to your good imagination to look around the world and judge for yourself that, which states are mindful of God, with a culture of righteous deeds, and provide these basic essentials to their citizens particularly to the minorities, protect the animals and the environment in order to fulfil the commandments of God?

Deeds On the Day of Judgement. I will now conclude with the verses of the Qur'an about the essence of good deeds during our life with regards to the Day of Judgement.

> *'Whoever has done a good deed will have ten times credit, and whoever has done a bad deed, it will equal to one only, and they will not be wronged'.* **(Qur'an 6:160)**

> *'The one whose scales of good deeds are heavy will have a delightful life, but the one whose scales of good deeds are light will have his home in a bottomless Pit'.* **(Qur'an 101:6-9)**

The above Suras were revealed in Mecca referring to some scenes of Resurrection and Judgement, where we will be held accountable for our deeds. The heavier scale of good deeds would lead to the paradise with the will of God. It is fair to say that, the prayers are must to worship God, indeed the good deeds being mindful of God are the essence of worship and purpose of our life.

Human is to Err. Being mindful of God and do good deeds, does not mean that we become angels who do not have free-will like us and are bound to do good by the will of God. We must remain human, and expect others to be the same, to make mistakes and even blunders during our life. As long as we do not hurt others deliberately and repeatedly as a way of our life, we should always be hopeful of forgiveness by God. Our God is most merciful, and forgiving on repentance, as revealed in the Holy Qur'an 4:25,31, 5:74, 9:102,104, 11:90, 15:49, and 85:14. We should trust God as a most merciful, loving and forgiving God who knows our intentions. Making our life and other lives happy, cheerful, fruitful and delightful will make God happy, and not making it miserable for ourselves and awkward for others.

Given below is a list of just a few examples about being, 'mindful of God and do good deeds.' But what about those who do evil deeds as a way of their life? I leave it to your choice to wish as you wish to, 'but what about those?'

Bless to those men who treat their mothers, sisters, wives, and daughters with respect, love and kindness, 'but what about those,' who do not care?
Bless to those wives, whose husbands are happy with them, they will have great respect in this world, will enter paradise without being asked any question, 'but what about those,' who do not care?
Bless to those who treat every human, especially the vulnerable and needy with love and kindness, 'but what about those,' who do not care?
Bless to those who wish others success, 'but what about those,' who wish to succeed but others to fail?
Bless to those who help others in good faith and forget, 'but what about those,' who prove ungrateful?
Bless to those who trust their friends, 'but what about those,' who betray their friends?
Bless to those who do justice and give prescribed alms (from their honest earnings) to the poor and needy, 'but what about those,' who do not care?
Bless to those who exhort people to truth and patience, 'but what about those,' who do not care?
Bless to those who use their power to serve the humanity, 'but what about those,' who abuse their power?
Bless to those who stand up to against the evils, 'but what about those,' who do evil or support the evil?

Bless and salute to those who treat animals with love and kindness, 'but what about those,' who are cruel to the animals?
Bless and salute to those governments and communities, who treat kindly and justly to the minorities, 'but what about those,' who are cruel and unjust to the minorities?
Bless to those who proclaim and work for peace, 'but what about those,' who are transgressors or terrorists (be it individuals, organisations or state terrorism)?
Bless to those who proclaim to promote better understanding with other communities, 'but what about those,' who invoke hatred against other communities or among the factions of their own community?
And last but not least:
Bless to those who are mindful of God and do good deeds, 'but what about those,' who pray to show off, and do evil deeds as a way of their life?

While the prayers are must to worship God, indeed, good deeds being mindful of God are the essence of worship, and purpose of our life. Let us therefore, '**race to do good**.'

Some Important Teachings for Muslims in the Qur'an

The practice of the religion of Islam is based upon the five pillars, which are the framework for worship and a sign of commitment to the faith. The five pillars includes, Kalama (Shahadah), daily prayers, fasting during the month of Ramadan, prescribed alms (Zakat), and Hajj (a pilgrimage to Mecca at least once in a lifetime by those men and women who can financially afford). Five pillars are meant to achieve the ultimate objective, 'be mindful of God and do good deeds.'

70

About Prayers (Qur'an 2:110, 2:177, 2:45, and 4:60). Prayers are not only necessary but essential duty to worship God, and ask for help from God alone. The most spiritual benefit of prayers to worship God is that it purifies the soul, and brings God's consciousness to do good deeds. In these verses, the Muslims are being commanded to keep up the prayers, pay the prescribed alms, keep promises, be steadfast in misfortune, give your wealth out of love of God to relatives, to orphans, to the needy and to the beggars. You must note that God is asking His humans to ask Him direct for help to establish a direct loving relationship with God, and that there is no middle man in between God and His humans. Prayers are neither the deeds nor the objective in itself but a spiritual means to achieve the objective, 'God's consciousness and do good deeds.' Prayers are a personal matter between each individual and God, and not a favour to any other person. Let us together bless those who offer prayers, are mindful of God, and as a result, 'do good deeds.' Such people are a great blessing for their family, friends, community and to the whole of humanity. It is very important to know the essence of the prayers, because only those who pray with the knowledge and understanding will take heed, as revealed below.

> *What about someone who worships during night, bowing down and standing, mindful of Hereafter, hoping for the Mercy of his Lord? Say, "Can those who know be equal to those who do not know?" Only those with understanding will take heed.* ***(Qur'an 39:9)***

Show of Prayers (Qur'an 29:2,4, 107:4-7). These verses reveal that: Do people think that they will be left alone on mere saying, 'We believe' and they will not be tested? Do

71

the evildoers think they can escape Us? So woe to those who pray but are heedless of their prayers; **those who make a show of it, and lack common kindness.**

Intoxication and Gambling. The first revelation of the Qur'an was in 610 AD when Prophet Muhammad (PBUH) was in Mecca. The Migration to Medina (Hijra) took place during 622 AD. The above mentioned three Suras were revealed to Prophet Muhammad while he was in Medina. As per these verses, the commandments for intoxication were revealed in three stages after over 13 years of the first revelation. The first revelation, 'the sin is far greater than the benefits,' is followed by 'do not pray if you are intoxicated, and finally forbidden' (Qur'an 2:229, 4:43, 5:90,91).

When the revelations of the Holy Qur'an started, it was a time of poetry and literature. It is known that there was a famous poet, by the name of Aba Mahajan Astaqafi, during the time of Prophet Muhammad, and he used to defend Islam in poetry with his good knowledge and understanding of the religion of Islam and its relationship with other communities. He had the honour of being a close companion of Muhammad and was highly respected in the community due to his distinguished character and good deeds. However, he used to drink alcohol regularly. The Prophet allowed him to continue being in his company during his lifetime, and he also continued being in the close company of Caliph Abu Bakar and Omer, despite not giving up drinking alcohol. The poet being mindful of God must have had a strong belief and trust in the mercy and forgiveness of God, to do what he was not supposed to do.

About Sins and Salvation. We have known from the ancient history, that the human has always been concerned about his sins and the salvation in the life hereafter. Human is to err. He will make mistakes, blunders and commit sins; however there is always a chance for his repentance and forgiveness by God. Let us have a look at the guidelines in the Qur'an.

Qur'an 4:48. '*Surely God does not forgive associating partners with Him. Anything else He may forgive if He wishes to.*'

Qur'an 6:164, and 35:18. '*Each soul is responsible for its own actions; no soul will bear the burden of another.*'

Qur'an 103. '*By the time, Verily man is in loss, except for those who have faith, **do righteous deeds**, urge one another to the truth, patience and tolerance.*'

Please note that the above Sura 103, 'about the salvation,' does not include the prayers and other rituals, because they are means to achieve the objective and not the objective itself, whereas the righteous deeds to please God are the essence of worship. The focus of this verse is upon, '**righteous deeds,** truth, patience and tolerance' however the prayers and other rituals are not only necessary but essential to praise, worship, and ask help from God alone, provided it leads to, 'be mindful of God and do righteous deeds.'

About Factions/Sects. Let us have a look at the guidelines in the Holy Qur'an:

Qur'an 3:103,105. '*Hold fast to God's rope all together; do not split into Sects. Do not be like those who, after they have been given clear revelation, split into sects and fall into a dispute: a terrible punishment awaits such people.*'

***Qur'an 6:159,160,164**. 'Those who have divided their religion into many sects, (O My Apostle) you have nothing to do with them. Their case rests with God and He will declare to them about their deeds. Whoever comes with a good deed will get ten times reward and whoever comes with a bad deed will be repaid only that one evil, and they will not be wronged. You will all return to God and He will make clear to you about your differences.'*

God has strictly forbidden and warned Muslims not to divide into factions, which is the most serious offence in Islam for the obvious reasons which can be seen with results of hatred and even killing each other, despite minor differences. Those who divide into sects despite the warning, God has shown His displeasure, but also revealed that, 'whoever comes with good deeds will be rewarded and will not be wronged. You will all return to God and He will make clear to you about your differences.' As I understand it, because they are all seeking guidance from the Holy Qur'an as they inherited from their ancestors to understand it, their righteous deeds will be rewarded by God and will not be wronged. The essence of these revelations are that, God alone is the Judge on the final day, He only knows the intentions, and He may reward as He wishes, which we will find out only when we all return to God. As long as they are mindful of God and do good deeds, there should be no friction with other factions, however, when it becomes politically motivated and leads to hatred and killing each other, they fail to realise that the factions are not above the religion. I sincerely feel that they are all very good Muslims, but misled by some of their leaders who are highly professional to invoke hatred against other factions. The solution lies in the awareness of the public about the real essence of the Holy Qur'an, so that the public condemns such leaders who invoke hatred against each other.

Misconceptions about Islam

It is to note that the original language, in which the religions were revealed, when translated or interpreted into other languages, will be open to different opinions. It is therefore important to understand the overall context of the message rather than an isolated verse or text which can be misleading. I have therefore provided the explanation about some of the important issues which lead to the misconceptions about Islam.

Islam is a Religion of Peace and Tolerance. Let us see the guidelines in the Qur'an.

Had your Lord willed, all the people on earth would have believed, one and all. Can you force people to become Muslims? **(Qur'an 10:99)**

God does not forbid you to deal kindly and justly with anyone who did not fight you in the matter of religion, nor drove you out of your homes. God loves those who do justice. **(Qur'an 60:8)**

Islam preaches peace and tolerance as a way of life for the Muslims. The height of peace and tolerance in Islam can be best described with the guidelines even during the war, where the objective is not to win the war, but to win the peace. Whereas the general guidelines are not to be transgressors against any community, Muslims are under strict orders to fight back the aggressors, and never surrender. There are revelations about a small group of those Jews and Christians who were creating mischief against Muslims, and not referred to the whole community. There are other verses applicable to the Pagans, idolaters, which must not be used against the People of Book. Some elements pick up such verses from the Qur'an out of context to build on it their theory of war and violence in Islam, a few examples are explained below.

Guidelines about War and Peace in the Qur'an. Islam these days is associated with the name of Jihad and terrorism, whereas it is the religion based upon peace, tolerance, right to self defence, strictly forbids terrorism and commands Muslims to combat terrorism. There is no word Jihad or sword to be found in the Qur'an. However, the proper Arabic word is Juhada, mentioned in the Qur'an which means to strive and struggle against evils in the society, against oppression, transgressors, and also in the battlefield to fight back the aggressor to achieve the ultimate objective of peace. Let us read and try to understand the revelations in the Qur'an on this subject, which gives a guideline to the Muslim state to derive their strategy, tactics and principles of war and peace.

Qur'an 2:190,192-195, 4:74,75, 90,91, 5:32, 8:15,61, and 9:4,6,40. These verses were revealed when the Muslims were established for the first time as a state in Medina, the laws to govern the Muslim community, to fight back the aggressor in self defence, and how to combat terrorism.

Killing any innocent person, regardless of race, religion, colour or gender, even during the war, is a major sin in Islam.

Transgression is totally forbidden.

The Muslim Army Commanders at all levels have to ensure during the battle, the safety and protection of the enemies' persons who are not party to fighting including unarmed men, women, the elderly, children, the sick and wounded. And also those who were involved in fighting and then surrender or stop fighting must be provided safety and protection.

It is the duty of every Muslim to defend themselves to fight back the aggressor, and to help those who call for help to fight back the aggressor like in Palestine and Kashmir.

If anyone commits aggression against you, you are allowed to attack him as he attacked you. If you are attacked and the enemy withdraws and offers peace, peace is always preferred.

God does not allow you to continue with the fight, if they stop, you must stop. Do not overstep the limits.

Honour the treaties.

Provide a safe place to those who seek protection.

Do not surrender, God rewards both, whether killed or victorious.

In view of my war experience, I have interpreted the above guidelines of the Qur'an about the war/battle for a Muslim state. The broad outline strategy of the war in Islam is to win the peace, and not the war. Transgression and killing any innocent person is a major sin. We must defend against aggression, and help who call for help to fight back the oppressor. There is a general feeling among the Muslims that we are allowed self defence only and perhaps to confine by fighting the battle from the trenches till we are attacked, which is not the case. Self defence means neither to be the aggressor to initiate the war nor to be the cause of it. But if attacked, or likely to be attacked beyond any reasonable doubts, the Qur'an gives the authority to attack as a pre-emptive strike or attack like the enemy attacked, keeping in mind all the time that the peace is always preferred, and not to overstep the limits. Peace is not acceptable if offered by the enemy while he is occupying a part of Muslim territory. While it is allowed to defend within this concept, there are many strings attached to it in the terms of restrictions and prohibitions mentioned above, which the Muslim Military Commanders at all levels must religiously follow.

Let us see how the guidelines in the Qur'an will be applicable in the modern time of today. A state will usually have Rangers, Scouts or similar kinds of force deployed on her borders. Such forces are not normally equipped with major weapons, but only the small arms. Their main role is to keep an eye on the borders, and give early warning by occupying defences, observation posts and patrolling to cover the gaps. The Army which has already prepared their defences on or near the borders may or may not be deployed in their defensive positions, but are ready to occupy at a short notice. The Air Force remains vigilant in the air, and by use of their Radar systems to keep an eye on the enemies' violation of Air Space or a surprise attack. The Naval Force similarly remains alert to counter any enemy threat from the sea. When the hostilities break out or are likely to break out, the regular forces would mobilise and occupy their defences. In addition to the defences, every Army has striking forces depending upon their resources to launch attacks to capture a territory and kill or capture the enemies' troops. The element of surprise plays a very significant role during the war, and an attack without any formal declaration may catch the opposite side unguarded and hence prove successful. A Muslim Army is allowed to launch a pre-emptive strike, provided it is confirmed beyond any reasonable doubt that the enemy has mobilised or is in the process of mobilising his forces with a view to attack us. Let us see in case the enemy attacks and how to retaliate.

In case of minor border skirmishes and Air Space violations by the enemy, it is our responsibility not to escalate the situation which may result in a major war. The patience and tolerance is to be observed, however the enemy should not be allowed to consider our patience as a sign of weakness. If the repeated severe warnings to the enemy do not work and he continues to violate the ceasefire, then you must retaliate proportionately. If the enemy attacks in strength, and it is part of the best strategy and tactics to attack, we must attack with all the possible resources at our disposal. Please note that, while the striking forces are busy in fighting the offensive battle, there are always troops on the ground in defence as well. It would also include Commando troops operating behind enemy lines, either dropped by air or infiltrating to carry out the interdiction missions such as Raids and Ambush. If the enemy stops and offers peace, we must stop and accept peace despite it maybe being advantageous for us to exploit the enemies' weakness. During such a situation, Islam does not allow to continue fighting to avoid further killing. The commanders at all levels must be trained and commanded to avoid collateral damage, and ensure that their troops do not kill any innocent person, do not harm civilians, but must protect and provide them with safety. Also, every soldier must be trained so that those enemy troops who surrender, or are injured and unfit to fight, must be provided safety/treatment and protected. Similarly, the pilots must strictly adhere to strike only the military targets and not the civilians. During the war, most of the casualties are caused by the aerial bombardment, the missiles, and the Artillery fire. The Muslim Artillery Commander has to ensure that his guns do not fire into the enemy civilians' area, even if the enemies' guns are firing on our civilians. Sometimes, it may be the best part of the strategy and tactics for an Army to fight a defensive battle, and within the defensive posture, he may launch counter attacks to recapture a lost territory, which is perfectly normal as part of the battle tactics. To sum up, it can be a purely defensive battle, or a combination of the defence, withdrawal and attack, depending upon the strategy and tactics. The Battle of Trench, where Meccans attacked Medina was a classic defensive battle in which Meccans lost with heavy casualties and were forced to withdraw. Muslims did not exploit their weakness to pursue the depleted, disorganised and demoralised Meccan attackers, to avoid further killing. The Battle of Tabuk, led by the Prophet himself, is an example of a pre-emptive strike, because the Byzantine emperor Heraclius had mobilised her forces on the Assyrian border for the conquest of Arabia. The Muslim Army marched towards the enemy as far as Tabuk to face the enemy rather than wait till they physically attacked. The strategy worked because the enemy forces preferred to disperse in the face of a large number of dedicated Muslim troops. The Muslim Army did not exploit the situation to fight the enemy but withdrew to avoid bloodshed, and instead the war, the peace was won. Consequently many Arab tribes abandoned the Byzantine Army and joined the Muslims. The rule of Muslims spread to other parts of Arabia, and the People of Book were not only protected, but free to practice their own religions.

Guidelines about 'Combating Terrorism' in the Qur'an

Terrorism is strictly forbidden, however there are revelations in the Qur'an to combat terrorism. Please note that the Qur'an refers to the terrorist activities as FITNA (persecution), as explained below:

Killing any innocent person, regardless of race, religion, colour or sex is a major sin in Islam. **(Qur'an 5:32)**

Do not kill any life God has made sacred except by right. **(Qur'an 6:151)**

Uphold justice and bear witness to God. **(Qur'an 4:135)**

Read, Recite and Proclaim, in the name of Lord Who created you. It is applicable both for men and women. **(Qur'an 96:1-5)**

Qur'an 2:190,195, 8:72, and 9:5. These Suras were revealed in Medina. The persecution from the tribes of Mecca was in its height, and during the four sacred months, the fighting is prohibited in Mecca. The Muslims were not sure whether to fight back to defend themselves or not. These revelations made it clear to the Muslims that they must defend themselves, and in the process kill them, drive them out from where they drove you out, fight them till there is no more persecution, because persecution is worse than killing. But if the enemy stops fighting, there can be no more fighting except against those who continue to fight. Also, it was revealed that those who ask for help against persecution, you must assist them except those with whom you have treaties. However the Muslims did not immediately declare the war, they gave an ultimatum that when the four sacred months are over, Muslims will wage a war on them.

It is important to note that even in this situation where the Muslims are allowed to fight back to defend themselves, there are many strings attached to it in the form of restrictions and prohibitions with a view to protect the innocent, avoid bloodshed, and achieve peace. Terrorism is an unlawful killing, and it is more serious than the war because the terrorists operate within the public. Like a fish cannot survive without water, similarly the terrorists cannot survive without the public, whether it is individual, organisation or state terrorism. Therefore the public must have the knowledge and the awareness of the message of the Qur'an, that it is a major sin, and the public must use all the possible means and resources available to defeat the terrorists. Islam awards the most serious penalties for such people involved in terrorist activities to include killing or causing damage to humans or property, planning, conspiring, recruiting, instigating others, assisting, concealing information and supporting such individuals and organisations.

As a matter of fact, the guideline to combat terrorism in Islam starts to tackle the root cause of the problem in the first place, which is injustice to a group or community and those deprived of their basic human rights. It ensures to provide basic human rights, educate people to raise awareness, and provide opportunities and justice. The public should therefore not support such corrupt governments who are the cause of injustice, discrimination, and fail to provide opportunities and basic human rights, to avoid people getting frustrated to the extent that they resort to terrorist activities.

You must have noticed that the Qur'an prefers peace even during a battle situation and is very much considerate even towards enemies' fighting troops who stop fighting, or who are injured, and their civilians. Transgression is totally prohibited. However, to fight back against the aggressor, the guidelines are very clear, 'fight back bravely with all the resources at your disposal, and do not surrender.' It is fair to conclude that Islam is a religion of peace and tolerance, and can be best described as **'peace acquired through complete submission to God's will.'**

Fundamentalist. Let us have a look at the guidelines in the Holy Qur'an:

Had your Lord willed, all the people on earth would have believed, one and all. Can you force people to become Muslims? **(Qur'an 10:99)**

God does not forbid you to deal kindly and justly with anyone who did not fight you in the matter of religion, nor drove you out of your homes. God loves those who do justice **(Qur'an 60:8)**

We have made you Muslims into a just community **(Qur'an 2:14)**.

The latter verse means literally a 'Middle Nation or a Religion of Moderation,' to live with other societies.

O Believers, do not abuse those false gods they worship, lest they also abuse God in their revenge and ignorance. **(Qur'an 6:108)**

Forbids arguing with the People of the Book but in a decent manner. **(Qur'an 29:46)**

I do not want to elaborate on the dictionary meanings of fundamentalist, because the people in general take the

83

negative meanings of this word, so I will explain it accordingly. There are fundamentalists in each community. I can categorise the People of Book of two kinds, the **'Rightly Guided and Misguided.'** Following the fundamentals of your religion is a very good thing which includes regards for all other communities, promote peace and harmony and not to be awkward and invoke hatred against other communities. As per the above verses, the Qur'an strictly forbids Muslims arguing with the People of Book, but in a decent manner, with wisdom and reasoning with the knowledge, only to convey the message, and not to dictate or control. The People of Book, have an honourable status in the Qur'an, which is important for every Muslim to understand and give it due respect and regards. There are different messages for others (idolaters and pagans), and we must not mix up and use it against the People of Book, which is a serious breach of the commandment of God. The verse above, for example, Qur'an 6:108, refers to the Pagans who used to worship false gods, which must not be referred to the People of Book. Islam preaches kindness to all the people regardless of the religion, unless anyone fights you in the matter of religion or drives you out of your home. The most appropriate example is about Prophet Muhammad who always respected and treated kindly his uncle Abu Talib, though he did not embrace Islam, and the Prophet was so upset on his uncle's death that it is known as the year of grief. It goes to prove that the belief is the personal matter between a person and God Almighty, whereas the respect for humanity is the very fundamental consideration in Islam.

It is the duty of every Muslim to proclaim and practice that Islam is basically a moderate religion, commands Muslims to live in harmony with all other communities of any religion and forbids excesses in our way of life. It is also the duty of every Muslim, hence the Muslim community, to control and condemn such misguided Muslims who invoke hatred against other communities or within the community. It is equally applicable to the Jewish and Christian communities to control and condemn their misguided people. The most beautiful guideline for Muslims is the last Sermon of Prophet Muhammad (PBUH). After praising and thanking God (a very small brief below), he said:

"Hurt no one so that no one may hurt you. Remember you will indeed meet your Lord, and that He will indeed reckon your deeds. All mankind are from Adam and Eve, a white has no superiority over a black, nor a black has any superiority over white, except by piety and good deeds."

Muslims Living in a Non Muslim State. Let us see the guidelines in the Qur'an.

You who believe, fulfil your obligations. **(Qur'an 5:1)**

Fulfil any pledge you make in the name of God, and do not break your oaths after you have solemnly confirmed them, because you have made God your surety. **(Qur'an 16:91,92)**

And if they seek your help against religions, it is your duty to help them, but not against a people between whom and you there is an agreement. **(Qur'an 8:72)**

The above revelations are self explanatory that the Muslims living or visiting a non Muslim state are under their religious obligation to abide by the law of the land. However, it does not mean, 'not to raise your voice against the act of aggression committed by the state or to give your honest opinion about the matters of the state you are a citizen of.' It simply means you are a law abiding Muslim citizen of the state you live in.

Status of Women in Islam

I have listed a few verses from the Holy Qur'an about the status of women in Islam (Qur'an 2:187,228,231, 4:3,19, 96:1-5, 17:23-24, 30:21, 65:6, and 96:1-5).

It is not lawful for a Muslim man to marry a woman against her will, and a good Muslim must treat his wife kindly. Husband and wife are like each other's garments. The love between husband and wife is a sign of God. The women shall have rights, just as they have responsibilities. Islam is the only religion to say that marry only once, though a Muslim man is allowed to marry up to four women. The most important requirement is to do justice and be equitable to all, which is almost an impossible challenge. The Muslim men have to be mindful of God, who monitors the deeds of all, so the requirements of justice to be met, are being monitored. This is the reason that there is a warning that, if you think you will not be able to meet the requirement of justice, than marry only once. Besides it is a hard job, probably it is the fear of not meeting the requirement of justice that most of the Muslim men marry only once.

The first Sura revealed in the Qur'an starts with 'read, recite and proclaim in the name of Lord who created you.' This commandment is applicable both to men and women. We are also being reminded how our parents looked after us when we were little. We are instructed to provide the highest level of respect, regards, care and love to our parents, and mother comes first. The Muslims are also well familiar with some of the very common Hadith as below.

The Prophet was asked, who in this world deserves the maximum respect, love and compassion? The Prophet replied three times, your mother. On the fourth time, he replied, then your father! Paradise lies beneath the feet of your mother. A wife whose husband is happy with her, she will enter paradise without being asked any questions!

Women in Islam have equal legal rights
There are equal legal rights in Islam for women, as per these verses revealed in the Qur'an, as regards the punishment, testimony of witness, and fair retribution is concerned. If someone accuses a chaste woman of fornication in Islam, there are four witnesses required as evidence, failing which the punishment of eighty lashes is awarded and the testimony of such a person afterwards is ever rejected (Qur'an 5:38, 21:178, and 24:2,4).

Nobody can deny the fact that the men and women are though born equal, they are different, physiologically, psychologically, biologically, physically, and they are different in their nature as given to them by the creator. Without a man there will be no woman and without a woman there will be no man, therefore they complement each other. The central message in Islam has a deep rooted psychology. The women in Islam as per the above mentioned verses in the Qur'an are actually placed in a driving seat, as a daughter, a sister, a wife and a mother. The most important commandment for the woman in Islam is to educate them. During Prophet Muhammad's time, the women were scholars of the highest imminent and he as well as his companions used to teach women especially and exclusively. The women took part in the political activities, like Hadrat Aisha, Samra Binte Wahaib, and Ume Warqa. There have been historical Muslim women leaders like Razia

Sultana, who ruled Saltanate of Delhi from 1236 to 1239, Shajarat al Durr, who ruled Egypt from 1250 to 1257, and Benazir Bhutto, twice elected Prime Minister of Pakistan. The women also took part in the battles during the time of the Prophet and women were encouraged to go to the mosque. The fact of the matter is that many Islamic countries are very much influenced by the cultures they inherited from their ancestors which is not in line with the teachings of Islam, though Islam gets the blame. The solution lies to acquire the knowledge of the Qur'an and comprehensive education for Muslim women to the highest level, to play an active role in the society, and be the educated mothers to lead our future generations. There is a definite need of Ijtihad (critical thinking) for a more progressive form of Islam with respect to the status of Muslim women, to earn for sure the blessings of God.

Jesus and Mary in the Holy Qur'an

Birth of Mary and about Zachariah her godfather (Qur'an 3:35-37). Mary's mother, Imran's wife, had dedicated her child growing in her womb entirely to God. When the child was born, as against the expectations of a boy, the child happened to be a girl, and was named Mary. Usually, as per the Jewish customs, the boys used to be dedicated to God, however when the girl Mary was taken to the Synagogue, there were so many candidates interested in adopting the beautiful girl, therefore it was mutually agreed to decide by drawing the lots, which fell to a priest named Zachariah. It was during the time of King Herod, King of Judea, that Mary was entrusted to the charge of Zachariah.

Mary was preferred by God over all the women of the world.

'The angel said to Mary: "Mary, God has chosen you, purified you, and preferred you over all the women of the world."' (Qur'an 3:42)

*Mary said, "How can I bear a son when no man has touched me, nor I have been unchaste," and Gabriel said, "your Lord said, 'It is easy for me, **We shall make him a sign to all people, a mercy from Us.** And so she conceived him and retired to a distant place."' (Qur'an 19:20-21)*

Infant Child Jesus (PBUH) Speaks to Defend His Mother about His Miraculous Birth without a Father

*When God will say, "Jesus, son of Mary! Remember My favour to you and your mother, how I **strengthened you with the Holy Spirit**, when you spoke to people as an infant and at the age of maturity." (Qur'an 5:110)*

The Christians and the Muslims believe in the miraculous birth of Jesus from his virgin mother Mary. The Bible does not tell us about the infant child Jesus having spoken to defend his mother, while the Qur'an does. Both the Bible and the Qur'an, however, tell us about the obvious anger of her close family members (a close tribal society), when they learnt about the child without any male intervention. This must have had been an amazing miracle to protect Mary, and also a sign from God for people to believe in Jesus.

Divinity Denied. The Messiah, Jesus, son of Mary was only a Messenger of God (Qur'an 4:17 and 5:73,75).

Trinity Denied. Certainly those who say that God is the third of three are defying the truth. A painful punishment will befall those who persist'. (Qur'an 5:73)

On the Day when God assembles all the Messengers.

'When God will ask Jesus, son of Mary, "O Jesus, did you say to the people, 'take me and my mother for two gods beside God'? He will submit, 'May You be exalted!' How dare I say to that which I had no right to say. If I had said this, You must have known it. I told them 'Worship God, my Lord and your Lord'. If you punish them, they are your servants, if You forgive them, You are the Almighty.'"
(Qur'an 5:116-118)

Foretells the coming of Muhammad ^(PBUH) under the name of Ahmad ^(PBUH). In this verse Jesus said to the People of Israel that, besides confirming the Torah which was revealed before him, he gives them good news of a Messenger to come, whose name will be Ahmad (Qur'an 61:6).

Recall, when God said, "Jesus, I will take you back and raise you up to Me. I will purify you of the disbelievers, and till the Day of Resurrection, I will make those who follow you superior to those who disbelieved you. Then you shall all return to Me and I shall judge between you concerning your differences." **(Qur'an 3:55)**

God Raised up Jesus ^(PBUH). The Jews claimed that they killed Jesus and crucified him, these Suras reveal:

'We have killed the Messiah, Jesus, son of Mary, The Messenger of God; whereas they neither killed him, nor crucified him but it was made to appear like that to them. God raised him up towards himself' **(Qur'an 4:157,158)**.

90

Note. There is a major difference between the Christians and the Muslims on this verse of the Holy Qur'an. The Christians believe that there are prophecies about Jesus (PBUH) to be nailed on the Cross, crying for help to his Father in heaven, his clothes to be divided by casting lots as per the prophecies **(Psalm, 21:16-18, Isaiah, 53:7-9)**, and that is exactly what the people around that time witnessed, the prophecy being fulfilled. The Christians believe that Jesus died on the Cross, was raised by God to Himself after the resurrection, whereas the Muslims believe Jesus was raised by God to Himself before the crucifixion. During an interfaith dialogue with a Christian, he said that, 'Muslims are right to believe what is revealed to them, and the Christians are also right to believe what appeared like that to them according to the Qur'an. However, the people of the time did not witness Jesus being raised by God to Himself at the time of crucifixion, but they did witness Jesus being raised by God to Himself after the resurrection.'

The second coming of Jesus (PBUH). The Qur'an confirms the second coming of Jesus. 'Surely Jesus is a sign of the Hour' **(Qur'an 43:61)**. 'There is not any one of the People of Book who will not believe in Jesus before his death, and on the Day of Resurrection he will be a witness against them' **(Qur'an 4:159)**.

Relationship of the Muslim Community with the People of Book

Let us see the revelations of the Holy Qur'an about the relationship of the Jews, Christians and the Muslims. One third of the Qur'an is about the People of Book (Jews and Christians). The name of Muhammad is mentioned in the Qur'an only five times (four times as Muhammad and once as Ahmad), while Moses is mentioned 136 times and Jesus 25 times, peace be upon all of them. There is a separate Sura in honour of Mary, the mother of Jesus. Please note that, though Prophet Muhammad is mentioned by name only five times, throughout the Qur'an God has addressed to him in the revelations. While the Muslims believe in the previous Holy Scriptures, the Jews and Christians do not believe in the Qur'an and Prophet Muhammad ^(PBUH).

Relationship of the Holy Scriptures

*'We gave Moses the Book for those who do righteous deeds, giving details of everything clearly as guidance and mercy, so that they believe in meeting their Lord. This too is a truly blessed Book, follow it and be conscious of your Lord to receive mercy, lest you say, 'The Books were only sent down to two communities (Jews and Christians) before us and we were not aware of what they studied, or if the Book had been sent down to us, **we would have been better guided than them**.' (Qur'an 6:154-157)*

*'He has revealed the scripture down to you with the Truth, confirming the Books which were sent before: He revealed the **Torah and the Gospel earlier as a guide for people** and He has revealed to you, **the distinction between right and wrong.'** (Qur'an 3:3-4)*

*'We gave Moses and Aaron the Scripture that distinguishes **right from wrong, a Light and a reminder** for those who are mindful of God. This (Qur'an) too is a blessed Scripture We have sent down. Are you going to deny it?'* **(Qur'an 21:48)**

*'O People of the Book! Our Messenger has come to make clear to you much of that you **concealed of the Scripture.'** (Qur'an 5:15)*

*'How can you say, "We are wise, and the law of the Lord is with us," when, in fact, **the false pen of the scribes** has made it into a lie?' **(Jeremiah 8:8)***

The above revelations of the Holy Qur'an clearly define the relationship of the Holy scriptures that the previous Holy Books (Torah and the Gospel) are a guidance and light, and distinction between right and wrong for two communities (Jews and Christians), and this too (Qur'an) is a blessed Book. Also is revealed that, if the Book (Qur'an) had been sent down only to the Muslims, they may not say that, 'we are better guided than them.' It is also revealed that the People of Book have not preserved the records as revealed. Please note that Prophet Moses [PBUH] had also shown his grave concerns about the corruption of records in the Holy Bible, which was also confirmed after about 800 years by the Prophet Jeremiah [PBUH], as above.

Relationship between the Communities. Sura 5 is the cornerstone of the relationship of the Muslim community with the Jewish and Christian communities. This Sura takes its title, 'THE FEAST,' for which the disciples of Jesus asked him to pray to God, which is very well known as, 'the last feast of Jesus.' As a matter of fact, the Jews and the Christians with the common faith of Abraham (complete devotion to God) are encouraged in the Qur'an to practice their own religions. Let us try to understand these verses.

*'**Why do they come to you for judgement**, when they already have with them the Torah wherein is the judgement of Allah?' **(Qur'an 5:43)***

The above verse refers to a case about adultery committed by a Jewish man and a woman, who would have been stoned as per the Jewish law. People from the Jewish community came to the Prophet Muhammad ^(PBUH) for a ruling, and as per this revelation, the Prophet could use his discretion to judge or decline. However they had ulterior motives, that if the Prophet ordered the lashing, they will accept it, but if he ordered stoning, they will reject, simply looking for a better deal. Besides this case of adultery, there is an important message to understand in this verse, 'why do they come to you for judgement, when they already have with them the Torah wherein is the judgement of Allah.' It means that the Jews with the common faith of Abraham, 'islam' (complete submission/devotion to God) should follow their own law and path revealed in the Torah, the Book of Allah.

*'We revealed the **Torah with guidance and light.** In the Torah, We prescribed for the Jews: a life for life, an eye for an eye, a tooth for a tooth-------. Those who do not judge by that Book what God has revealed are the wrongdoers.' **(Qur'an 5:44,45)***

*'We sent after them Jesus, son of Mary, confirming the Torah which had been sent before him; We gave to him the **Gospel with guidance, light,** and confirmation of the Torah already **revealed as a guidance and light** for those who are mindful of God. And let the follower of the Gospel judge according to what God has sent down in it. And*

those who do not judge by what God has sent down are lawbreakers.' **(Qur'an 5:46,47)**

'And (O My Apostle!) We have sent down to you the Book (Qur'an) with **the message of truth,** *confirming the scriptures before it, and is* **a guardian over them**; *So judge between them what Allah has revealed to you.* **We have prescribed a law and a path to each of you**. *If God had so willed, He would have made you all one community, but He desired to test you through that which He has given to you,* **so race to do good**; *you will all return to God and He will make clear to you the matters you used to dispute about.'* **(Qur'an 5:48)**

'Say, 'People of the Book', you have no true basis unless you uphold the Torah and the Gospel, and that which has been sent down to you from your Lord . Surely for the Muslims, the Jews, the Sabians, and the Christians, **whosoever believe in God and the Last Day and do good deeds,** *shall have nothing to fear, nor shall they grieve.'* **(Qur'an 5:65, 66,68, 69)**

Note. It is fair to say that each community have no true basis unless they uphold their respective Holy Books.

Prayer Directions. *'Each community has its own direction to which it turns its face,* **'race to do good'**, *and wherever you are,* **God will bring you all together'** *(Qur'an 2:148).*

'For us are our deeds and for you are your deeds, so there is no need for any argument between you and us. God will

gather us together, and to Him we shall return'. **(Qur'an 42:15)**

'Let us arrive at common terms between you and us. Believe in one God, associate no partners with Him and worship none but Him alone'. **(Qur'an 3:64)**

It has been revealed in the above verses of the Qur'an that all the Holy Books are the guidance and light, and distinction between right and wrong for each community, and that they will be tested through that which has been sent down to them. God has commanded them to follow your own law and path, and whichever direction you offer your prayer, race to do good and God will bring you all together. The purpose of the life for all the three communities is that those who are mindful of God and do good deeds will be rewarded, have nothing to fear and will not grieve. About the differences it is revealed that you will all return to God and He will make clear to you the matters you used to dispute about.

The Holy Qur'an reveals to the Muslims to invite the People of Book to come to common terms with us, 'to believe in one God, associate no partners with Him and worship none but Him alone.' I therefore had an interfaith dialogue with some Christians based upon the guidelines of the Qur'an, the details are given under the heading, 'A Trial to Proclaim to the Christians.' A brief of the interfaith dialogue is appropriate to mention here for better understanding. The purpose of this dialogue was not to prove them wrong, but to understand each other, to convey the message and work together to race to do good. When I reminded them about our common terms, they said that, 'we believe in one God, we associate no partners with Him and worship none but

Him alone but we worship trinity (God the Father, the Son and the Holy Spirit), which are three characteristics of one and the same God. God visited our world in the human form of Jesus, as God Himself had revealed in the prophecies hundreds of years before the birth of Jesus which were fulfilled through Jesus.' I asked them about the Holy Spirit. They said, 'if we are mindful of God the Father, the Son and the Holy Spirit, we are guided by the Holy Spirit which means God is with us.' I asked, how do you know that you have got the Holy Spirit? They said, 'it inspires us to love and help all the humans regardless of their belief, love all other creatures of God, and love His environment, and make our life and the life of others cheerful, full of fun and excitement. If we do evil deeds as a way of life, Jesus will be hurt, we confess, as well as repent, and hope for forgiveness through Jesus.' I asked them about the trinity that, you believe in one God, associate no partners with Him and worship trinity which is not mentioned in the Holy Bible? They replied that, 'it is not about the word trinity in the Bible, it is the essence of the fulfilment of all the prophecies about Jesus, and what Jesus finally said after his resurrection 'Go therefore and make disciples of all nations, baptizing them in the name of the Father and of the Son and of the Holy Spirit', (Matthew 28:19). No one on earth has seen the Father. The son from the heaven has seen Him and bears witness of Him, doing His works and speaking His words. Therefore we Christians believe in one God, associate no partners with Him and worship trinity (God the Father, the Son and the Holy Spirit), which are the characteristics of one and the same God. Better we wait till the second coming of Jesus, and then he will make clear to us about the differences, meanwhile let us serve the humanity'.

Having tried to understand some Christians about our common terms, I reminded myself about the essence of the Holy Qur'an, which is God's consciousness (taqwa) or to be mindful of God, means God is with us, which inspires us to do good deeds, to love all humans regardless of their belief, other creatures and the environment, which would please God, and He will bless us with His guidance. If we do evil deeds as a way of our life, hate other humans, are cruel to other creatures, and abuse the environment, it will hurt God, and it means we lack God's consciousness. We confess, as well as repent and ask for forgiveness from God who is most merciful and forgiving and we trust that He will forgive us if He wishes to. Obviously major difference is about the faith.

During the interfaith dialogue, I also explained the revelations of the Holy Qur'an that, with the common faith of Abraham (complete submission/devotion to God), each community has been assigned a different law and path to follow. Like we Muslims believe in the Holy Bible and follow our own religion, you may also believe in Prophet Muhammad [PBUH] and the Holy Qur'an, with the common faith of Abraham [PBUH], and follow your own religion? They replied that, 'we can believe either in one or the other. To believe in the Qur'an means to disbelieve in the fulfilment of the prophecies about Jesus [PBUH], which were the physical acts witnessed by the people of the time. And we have always regarded Abraham as our father in faith (complete devotion to God), even before your Holy Qur'an.'

Another response from a Christian lady during an interfaith dialogue, she said that, 'Your Holy Qur'an is an amazing Book, and we all need to understand it with an open mind and in the overall context of the Holy Bible. As I understand it from your Holy Qur'an, we are all being tested in different ways through our respective revealed Scriptures, and each of us must sincerely follow our own Holy Book as we understand it. Indeed it strengthens my believe in Jesus to know that, no Muslim can be a Muslim unless he/she believes in Jesus Christ despite it is different to us according to the Holy Qur'an. As a mother, while I groom my children to believe in Jesus, I also make sure that they do not blame any other child or person for their belief, but to love and respect them to please Jesus. However, I will have to explain to my children particularly about our spiritual differences with Islam with a view to understand and respect each other. I trust that the Muslim mothers would also groom their children to follow their beautiful religion Islam, and have mutual respect for all others regardless of any religion. Surely our arguments, the attitudes of dictating and blaming each other will not please God, but as per your Holy Qur'an, 'race to do good, you will all return to God and He will make clear to you the matters you used to dispute about', will definitely please God'.

As I understand it
In view of the above, I can briefly summarise my understanding about the relationship of Muslims with the People of Book.

There are differences not only between these religions, but also among the factions of each religion, due to different interpretations and/or understandings of the Holy Books, which have been revealed by the same source, the Lord of the universe. The followers of these three religions have been commanded by the Lord that you will be tested in different ways through that which has been sent down to you. It is fair to say that because the Jews, Christians and Muslims seek guidance from their Holy Books to understand as their ancestors understood about the God and His commandments, therefore the case about all their differences rests with the source of the message which is God and God alone. Whether the matter of differences is among the factions of their respective religions, or between the other religions, God alone is the Judge, and He has revealed the solution, 'you will all return to God and He will make clear to you the matters you used to dispute about,' (Qur'an 5:48). A highly competitive race is on among the factions of each religion, as well as against each other religion, but unfortunately not a race to do good, but a race with their gloves off to fight out their differences about the interpretation and understanding of the Holy Books, perhaps they will race to do good when they all return to God.

It is also important to highlight that because the Jews and Christians seek guidance from their Holy Books, which the Muslims also believe in, their status for the Muslims will always remain as an honourable status of the People of Book, for all times to come. I can therefore sum up that, the relationship of the Jews, Christians and Muslims is not based upon what they are, or what they look like, or what their cultures are, or what their differences are, or whether they pray in a synagogue, church or mosque. It is indeed a spiritual relationship and supposed to be a bond of the Holy Books revealed by the same source, God, the Lord of the universe. God is the real bond of their relationship, which is neither limited to time nor geographical boundaries, the most spiritual bond to be mindful of God and race to do good, you will all return to God and He will make clear to you the matters you used to dispute about. (Qur'an 5:48)

About the Interpretations. Sometimes certain verses of the Holy Qur'an are misinterpreted, for example the verses below are commonly used and misinterpreted either wittingly or unwittingly, therefore let us try to understand the context of these verses before we proceed any further.

'If anyone seeks a religion other than islam (complete submission/devotion to God), it shall certainly not be accepted from him; and the world to come, he shall be one of the losers.' **(Qur'an 3:85)**

Please note that the word islam in the Arabic Qur'an means complete submission/devotion to God (faith), which is also referred to be the faith of Jews and Christians, as well as the faith of all the prophets before the revealed Books as mentioned above. It must not be mixed up with the religion Islam which means faith combined with the law and path that came into being upon the revelation of the Holy Qur'an. Let us now try to understand this verse (3:85) in the context, including just a verse previous to this.

*'Say (O Muslims), "We believe in God and in what has been sent down to us, and which was sent down to Abraham, Ishmael, Isaac, Jacob, and their offspring, and what has been given to Moses, Jesus and the prophets from their Lord. **We make no distinction between any of them. In the matter of faith, we have surrendered to God."'** (Qur'an 3:84)*

'In the matters of faith, *He has decreed for you the same commandment that He gave Noah, which We have revealed to you and which We enjoined on Abraham and Moses and Jesus: "Establish this faith and do not divide into factions within it."'* **(Qur'an 42:13)**

You will notice from the above two verses that the subject verse in the context is referred to the common faith, islam (complete submission/devotion to God) of all the previous prophets, before the Holy Qur'an was revealed, and it does not refer to the religion Islam (faith combined with the law and path).

*'Surely the true religion in the sight of God is islam (complete submission/devotion to God alone). So if they dispute with you, say, "**I have surrendered myself to God** and so have my followers." Ask those who were given the Book, as well as those without the Book, "**Do you too devote yourselves to God alone?" If they accept, they are truly guided,** but if they turn away, then your responsibility is to convey the message, and verily God is aware of His servants'. (**Qur'an 3:19,20**)*

The above Sura was revealed in Medina, which begins with the confirmation of previous Holy Books. The central message as above is, 'I have surrendered myself to God,' which is about the faith islam, 'those who completely devote to God are truly guided.' The People of Book are also supposed to have the faith of Abraham, complete devotion to God, hence it refers to the faith islam not the religion Islam.

Those who interpret the word islam, in the sense of the religion Islam which includes the faith and the law and path will set up a barrier between the People of Book and Muslims, and may also affect the interpretation of other messages in the Holy Qur'an about the People of Book. In view of the above the Jews, Christians and the Muslims with a common faith, each has been prescribed a different law and path to follow and they will be tested through that which has been sent down to them as per their respective Holy Books. (Qur'an 5:43-48)

'O you who believe, do not take the Jews and Christians as allies....'. **(Qur'an 5:51)**

The above verse, if understood in the context with other verses of the Qur'an 5:51-59, makes it clear that it is referred to a particular group of Jews and Christians, who were against the Muslim camp, and some of the Muslims out of fear turned to them for protection. Also it is referred to only those who ridicule or make fun of your religion.

Qur'an 3:118,119. These verses are not against a particular community as a whole but referred to **such outsiders** who like to see Muslims in ruin and suffer, and do not take such outsider as your intimates.

Qur'an 19:66-92. In 'Sura Mary,' named after the mother of Jesus, the claim about, 'Jesus the son of God' is certainly denied. Also revealed in this Sura are these verses about the denial and highest level of anger of God for the Pagans of Mecca who used to say that, 'the angels were the daughters of God.' Some Muslims wittingly or unwittingly misinterpret these verses and use them against the Christians who say about Jesus, 'son of God.' The Arabic word, 'walad,' we read in these verses means child or children (without gender), hence in the context, the anger of God is referred to the Pagans of Mecca and their claim that the angels were the daughters of God.

'Our Nearest Friends are Christians,' Reveals the Qur'an

'You are sure to find of all the people, the nearest in friendship to the Muslims are those who say, "We are Christians", these people are not proud and stiff necked, there are people among them who are open to learning and practice strict self discipline. When they listen to the message, they show their emotions and recognise the truth.' **(Qur'an 5:82,83)**

I have been puzzled in understanding the above verse of the Holy Qur'an for a very long time, because of the differences and the past history of the Christians and Muslims, but I was sure that there must be a great wisdom behind it. History also tells us that the followers of both the divine religions have failed to solve the problems of their own communities, let alone the problems of the whole of humanity. With this background, it was not very helpful to find a convincing logic of their friendship. However, the wisdom of God can only be found with the guidance of God, so I ignored all their differences and started to enjoy wishful thinking of their friendship. I focused upon the common grounds between them, particularly the near and dear to their hearts, which could be the master key of this message as I have understood and explained below.

First Ever Asylum in our World. I will take you back to the very start of the history of Muslims, the fifth year of preaching of Islam, when they were subjected to the worst persecution from the different tribes of Mecca. The first ever asylum of humans took place, when the Muslims (about 100) migrated to Abyssinia (now Ethiopia), to seek protection under a Christian king during the time of Prophet Muhammad (PBUH). The Muslims later returned from exile to their homeland Mecca with an understanding that they will be safe. They were instead subjected to even worse atrocities from the tribes of Mecca. The Muslims had to migrate a second time to Abyssinia, to seek asylum and protection under the Christian king. It is fair to conclude that the Muslims must have been protected and taken care of by the Christians during the first time of their migration, to return and trust in their protection for a second time. Needless to say these Christians had proved themselves trustworthy as friends and protectors to our ancestors at the very beginning of our history.

'Mary was preferred by God over all the women of the world. 'The angel said to Mary: "Mary, God has chosen you, purified you, and preferred you over all the women of the world."' **(Qur'an 3:42)**

The basis of the relationship of the two communities are the Holy Books, revealed from the same source, the God, the Lord of the universe. The common grounds between the Christians and the Muslims, which is near and dear to their hearts are the love of Jesus and Mary, though in their own ways, but the love is love. Mary has been preferred by God over all the women of the world, which is the height of a respectable status of mother Mary for the Muslims. I will therefore, from the very depth of my heart call, 'Mary, the mother of the Christians and Muslims.'

While the Jews rejected Jesus (PBUH), both the Christians and Muslims believe in the second coming of Jesus with the blessings about the solutions for the problems of humanity. Maybe God has blessed the Muslims and Christians to work together to establish peace and justice for all in our world, before the second coming of Jesus. Maybe the mother Mary has got some blessings for us, and also a stick in her hand like an angry mother, telling us, "Stop behaving like kids. Get out now. Go and work together to help those in need and in pain before Jesus comes." It is also important to clarify that, while the Christians and Muslims believe in the second coming of Jesus, there are differences as well. However, the common belief is that, the peace and justice will ultimately prevail in our disturbed world on the second coming of Jesus (PBUH).

We can never ignore the belief of the Jews who are also the grand children of our grand father Abraham (PBUH), and that they seek guidance from their Holy Bible revealed by the same source, the Lord of the universe. The Messianic Era according to the Jews is self explanatory, 'nation shall not lift up sword against nation, neither shall they learn war any more'. (Isaiah 2:4)

In view of the above, it is fair to say that, the Christians and Muslims should start preparing for the second coming of Jesus, which God may expedite through His mercy to fulfil His scripture and promise, provided we work together to serve the whole of humanity, and leave our differences till we all return to God. That is how I interpret the above verse of the Holy Qur'an about the friendship of Christians and Muslims in the larger interest for all in our world, particularly the interest of Non-Christians and Non-Muslims.

Proclaim

The following guidelines of the Holy Qur'an and the last Sermon of Prophet Muhammad (PBUH) must be kept in mind to perform this duty:

'Read, Recite, and Proclaim in the name of Lord, who created you....'. **(Qur'an 96:1-5)**

'O Prophet, proclaim to the people, which has been sent down to you from your Lord....'. **(Qur'an 5:67)**

'And had your Lord willed, all the people on earth would have believed, one and all. Can you force people to become Muslims?' **(Qur'an 10:99)**

'We have made you Muslims into a just community.' **(Qur'an 2:14)**

The latter verse means literally a 'Middle Nation or a Religion of Moderation', to live with other societies.

'God does not forbid you to deal kindly and justly with anyone who did not fight you in the matter of religion, nor drove you out of your homes. God loves those who do justice.' **(Qur'an 60:8)**

*'Do people think that they will be left alone on mere saying, "**We believe" and will not be tested?** Do the evildoers think they can escape Us?'* **(Qur'an 29:2,4)**

What about someone who worships during night, bowing down and standing, mindful of Hereafter, hoping for the

Mercy of his Lord? Say, "Can those who know be equal to those who do not know?" Only those with understanding will take heed.' *(Qur'an 39:9)*

The most beautiful guideline for Muslims about the essence of the Holy Qur'an is, 'the last Sermon of Prophet Muhammad (PBUH).' After praising and thanking God (a very small brief below), he said:

*"Hurt no one so that no one may hurt you. Remember you will indeed meet your Lord, and that **He will indeed reckon your deeds**. All mankind are from Adam and Eve, a white has no superiority over a black, nor a black has any superiority over white, **except by piety and good deeds."***

To proclaim is one of the most beautiful commandments which we need to understand particularly about its wisdom behind it. While it is the duty of every Muslim to proclaim, it is also the duty of every Muslim man and woman to acquire the knowledge and act upon it, before we proclaim to others that Islam is a religion of peace, tolerance, justice, and righteous deeds. Little knowledge is though dangerous, but you must have heard that, even if you know one word, you must proclaim. It is therefore a must to find about this one word, which plays a pivotal role to proclaim. This one word is, 'God,' Who has commanded Muslims to treat all other humans kindly and justly, unless they fight you in a matter of your religion or drive you out of your homes. This is the bottom line to proclaim and to identify the rightly guided or misguided Muslims. Indeed the responsibility to demonstrate the knowledge into practice (righteous deeds) mainly lies with the Muslims to establish that it works, like they say, **'the actions speak louder than words.'** The best example of practical demonstration of righteous deeds can be referred to the time of Prophet Muhammad ^(PBUH) and the rightly guided Caliphs. The present and past hatred and killing of each other by different factions of Islam is not a very good demonstration. The lack of protection (person, property and dignity), equality of human rights, opportunities, justice, the height of corruption, and the cruelty to animals in our Muslim countries are not a very good demonstration of being mindful of God and do good deeds. Most of the Muslims are deprived of their basic human rights and dignity. The majority who are God fearing people are helpless and also the victims in the hands of those who neither love nor fear God. The superstitious practices are part of the daily life of Muslims due to a lack of awareness about Islam. For all these things the image of Islam is being affected adversely. However, we are where we are, and I proceed to proclaim, because it is our duty to proclaim.

What to Proclaim

The central point to focus upon is that, 'the Qur'an is a word of God', and to proclaim as to why we Muslims believe what we believe. If someone can not or does not believe in the Holy Qur'an, there is no point in proving his/her religion wrong. This will help us to understand each other, learn to differ and race to do good. However, you will notice much more probing questions in a friendly atmosphere that I discussed during the dialogue with the Christians with a view to provide you more information and understanding as to why they believe what they believe, and why we Muslims believe what we believe.

The following verses in the light of many others mentioned in this book sum up the context of the message as a guideline to, 'what to proclaim' to the Christians:

'Say, "People of the Book", let us come to the **common terms***: we believe in one God, associate no partners with Him, and we worship none but Him alone.'* **(Qur'an 3:64)**

'"People of the Book", believe in this Book, this is also a blessed Scripture, it confirms the previous Books, and to confirm what was revealed to you to make things clear for you to follow your own religion.' **(Qur'an 4:47, 5:15,48, 6:91,92)**

'Say, "Surely for the Muslims, the Jews, the Sabians, and the Christians, whosoever believe in God and the Last Day and **do good deeds***, shall have nothing to fear, nor shall they grieve."'* **(Qur'an 5:69)**

'Whichever direction you turn to pray, **'race to do good'***, and wherever you might be, God will bring you all together.'* **(Qur'an 21:49)**

'We have prescribed a law and path to each of you. If God had so willed he would have made you all one community, but He desired to test you through that which He has given to you. So, **'race to do good.'** *You will all return to God and he will make clear to you the matters you used to dispute about.'* **(Qur'an 5:48)**

You will notice from the above verses that the central point of interfaith dialogue is to remind them about our common terms about the faith (believe in one God, associate no partners with Him and worship none but Him alone) and not about the law and path, because they have been prescribed a different law and path, as a different community (different religion). As we all know that the Muslims believe in the previous Holy Books and the prophets, the Jews and Christians do not believe in the Holy Qur'an and Prophet Muhammad [PBUH]. We are therefore supposed to proclaim that the Holy Qur'an is also a blessed Scripture, believe in it, it confirms the previous revelations, and to confirm what was revealed to them to make things clear for them, to follow their own religion. We need to understand each other about, 'why we believe what we believe,' and that the purpose of our life is the same to, 'be mindful of God and do good deeds.' Both of us believe in the Last Day of judgement where we all will be held accountable for our deeds, so let us race to do good and leave our differences till we all return to God.

Islam is a religion of peace and tolerance. Islam is a religion of moderation, justice, equality of human rights and dignity, peace and tolerance which we should try our best to demonstrate, proclaim and also be able to clear up the misinterpretations and misconceptions about Islam as already explained above.

The Qur'an is Word of God. The Holy Qur'an has the power to prove that it is the word of God, provided we understand and explain with knowledge and wisdom. It is quite obvious that if someone does not believe in the Qur'an as the word of God, the messages revealed in the Qur'an will have no effect upon him/her. I have therefore focused upon it the most, as explained above under the heading, 'The Holy Qur'an.'

Let us race to do good
The Christians and Muslims are the two biggest religions, they can raise their level to lead the world together to

establish peace and justice, and reach the victims of our world regardless of race, religion, colour or gender. I therefore recommend a **Four Step Guide** to proclaim :

Step 1. *'Our nearest friends are Christians',reveals the Holy Qur'an.*
Step 2. *Islam is a religion of Peace and Tolerance.*
Step 3. *The Qur'an is Word of God.*
Step 4. *Let us race to do good.*

How to Proclaim

Let us first have a look at the guidelines from the Qur'an about 'How to Proclaim' to Christians.

> *'Forbids arguing with the People of the Book but in a decent manner and instructs the Muslims to say; "We believe in what was sent down to us and in what was sent down to you; our God and your God are one and the same."'* **(Qur'an 29:46)**

> *'Say to them, **"Produce your evidence**, if you are truthful. In fact, **whoever surrenders himself to God and do good** will have their reward with their Lord, and they shall have nothing to fear nor shall they grieve."'* **(Qur'an 2:111,112)**

The above Suras emphasise the evidence of truth, complete surrender to God (faith islam, not religion Islam), and to do good deeds (each following their own law and path).

> *'There is no compulsion in religion. You are only to convey the message, not to control, dictate or force them to believe.'* **(Qur'an 2:256, 35:23, 88:21)**

There are two simple choices of how to Proclaim: 'Isolate/Confrontation,' or 'Integrate/Friendship!' A confrontational approach is aimed at proving them wrong by Intellectual Judo, which I am sure is against the guideline of the Qur'an, that you are forbidden to argue with them, except with decent manners, using your wisdom. I have chosen a friendly approach, to provide proof that the Qur'an is a true blessed Scripture. This friendly approach has the concept of, 'Integrate to Proclaim, and Proclaim to Integrate,' with a view to conveying the message and in the process to promote understanding, clear the misconceptions about Islam, and to work together for a greater cause to establish peace and justice in our world.

You must retain the control to proceed with the step-by-step guide, and confirm at suitable intervals that he/she has understood what you have explained and if need be clarify it. Ask their feelings at the end of each step, and answer any query about misconception or misinterpretation, before you proceed any further. If there is a query about the differences, say, I will come back to it later and proceed further. It may be that such query is clarified in your subsequent presentation. However you must answer the pending queries towards the end. Make sure that in the process, you are supposed to better the relations, and not to make it worse.

A Trial to Proclaim. So far, I was satisfied with, 'What to Proclaim and How to Proclaim,' but it was all theoretical, so I decided to carry out a practical trial, before I recommend others to do the same. I had no doubts that it will be quite a challenging mission, and I should be ready to respond to all sorts of questions, whether I like it or not. Somehow, I was confident to take this challenge, because I was sure that I will adhere to the guidelines of the Qur'an. I embarked upon the venture of making use of my limited knowledge as a student of history and comparative religion studies. I started to share my knowledge with others, and I approached mostly the people I knew, and I was pleased that the people were happy to share their knowledge. I had a dialogue and discussions mostly with the Christians, the Muslims, and surprisingly some others who are impressed with the faith of Abraham (complete submission/devotion to God), but did not believe in the law and path of religions. They preferred to be called as, 'the Children of God', in the sense of utmost respect and love for God who is our creator.

A Trial to Proclaim to the Children of God

I started this trial with some of the people (male and female) who, 'believe in one God, associate no partners with Him and worship none but Him alone without any law and path.' They believe that, there can be no monopoly over God, or being mindful of God and/or to do good deeds that, each of the three religions claim. They firmly believe that, all humans are supposed to be the children of God in the sense of utmost love and respect for God who is our creator, and not the slaves of the laws of the religions. They said that, honestly speaking, when we study the life of Abraham, Moses, David, Jesus, and Muhammad (peace be upon all of them), we cannot escape but to fall in love with all of them. With due respect to all, we have been impressed the most with the faith of Abraham, who had blind faith in God, and he is the true role model for the whole of humanity. I have given below their reasons under separate headings, and towards the end, I have given my response to their views. It will be a real challenge of patient hearing, but I am sure that I will be able to respond decently with the proof, wisdom, reasoning and knowledge as revealed in the Holy Bible and Holy Qur'an.

God and the Holy Scriptures. Some of the Children of God said that by using their common sense, they believe that there is definitely a creator who created this world and only the creator of this world knows who created the creator and so on. They said it is also in our interest to believe in one God, because it is the only way to establish the relationship of brothers in humanity, and in faith. One of the main reasons is they reckon that in order for a commandment to be fulfilled or obeyed, the message has to be clear, it has to be the same for the whole of humanity, which is the sole responsibility of the one who gives the commandment, i.e. God. There is too much confusion about the message for a common man to understand, interpret thus to implement, as it is obvious from these three different religions and their factions. Each religion has different stories about Abraham in their respective Holy Books, and they should at least agree about their common forefather for their own credibility. In order to make Sarah and Isaac superior to Hagar and Ishmael, they have involved Abraham and God into it. Abraham never ever could discriminate between his wives and the sons, and how could God discriminate to whom we look up to for justice and equality. The Jews and Christians claim that Isaac was the son offered to God as a test of sacrifice, whereas the Muslims claim about Ishmael. Moses himself had shown concerns about the Scribes corrupting the records, which was confirmed by Prophet Jeremiah. The Qur'an has also mentioned about the corruption of records of the previous Scriptures. The only Scripture in the original form is known to be the Qur'an, but look at the different interpretations and understandings of the followers of the Qur'an, whose factions are fighting and killing each other. They firmly believe that the greatest man who ever lived on our planet was Abraham, as a role model of faith and whosoever has faith of Abraham is the seed of Abraham, the seed in faith, and not the seed in a biological sense to enslave others. With the faith of Abraham, God will guide the people to work out their own law and path according to the time and their changing circumstances, and that is called the faith of Abraham, which is to completely surrender to God Almighty for guidance, use your common sense and decide a way of life with the consent of the majority. The simple test for the followers of these religions is to judge them not by the numbers of people in the synagogue, church or mosque, but if they provide security, justice and opportunities to their own people, care for the minorities and the innocent animals, and do not transgress against other countries. None of these three communities would qualify all the very basic tests of the humanity. You will find good examples of justice, equal opportunities for their own people and care for the minorities, where the people are not too rigid in their religion, but have evolved as a civilised society. There are sad examples of mistreating the minorities, simply because they are too much in love with their own religion, which shows they neither love God nor fear God. With the faith in one God and no desert laws, you will love all humans regardless of their faith or no faith, which would ultimately encourage every human to believe in one God and live in peace and harmony with mutual respect for each other.

Some of the Children of God believe that in this vast world, these three religions started by one family in a small part of a desert, where there was bitter tribal factions, ignorance, lawlessness and corruption of the highest order. With due respect to all of them, it looks like one family business which started with a view to keeping it all in the family and has grown into a monopoly of our world, but the family is torn apart. God raised prophets only from one family whose intentions to gain power and control are clear that, if you believe in God, obey God and then obey His Messenger, love your parents, love your neighbours, do good deeds, and you are in it. Their contractors and sub contractors continue to control the minds of the people with the same concept, and exploit them. It means that, you cannot believe in God, worship God, be mindful of God, love your parents, love your neighbours and do good deeds, unless you are part of only their camp. The different factions of these religions do not worship God in the same synagogue, church or mosque speaks for itself as man made laws according to them. Also it goes to prove that, there is no one way to worship God who knows our intentions and can understand any language when we call Him from the core of our heart.

They highlighted the history of desert tribes that, in order to rule such lawless people of the desert, it was a good invention of man-made laws and commandments like a tooth for a tooth and an eye for an eye, as per Jews law, if someone hits you on one cheek, offer him the other one as per Christians law, and chop off the hands of a male or female thief as per Muslims law, all of which are impractical and/or barbaric man-made laws using the name of God. No religion is following these desert laws completely, which speaks for itself that it is not practical. It is more of a fiction with a view to control the minds of the people to gain power and control by using the name of God, scaring innocent people about hell and giving them an incentive of heaven. God's consciousness is the essence, which cannot be achieved through fear, but love, because those who love God, fear the most as well. They have gone too far to control the minds of the people as expected from the desert laws of the time, about the dress codes, cannot make love and have to even breathe according to their laws. They said that all three religions claim that humans are equal, whereas they are all highly discriminatory especially against the poor class and women. They said that slavery was the most common practice during the time, and none of these religions abolished slavery, despite preaching equality of human rights and dignity for humanity. They said that, look at the dress codes particularly for the poor women, which is typical of a desert law. It was a custom within the Greek society before the revealed religions, which was adopted as the commandment of God to suppress the women, whereas the modality of a woman as we experience in our life is inside and not outside her head. They said that all the three religions preach about peace, but peace only on their terms, provided humans are sheep of their flock. They said that history is a witness that the peace of our world has been mainly destroyed by these religions in the past, who are preaching peace in the name of God. These three religions have made humans into robots to exploit, since he is weak, has fear of the unknown as part of human nature. They are using religion as a recruitment agency to recruit people to fight each other, each claiming that there is only one God and their Scripture is the only one accepted to God.

Some of the Children of God believe that we are the creatures like all other creatures in this world except that we are created as the most intelligent and naughty creature of all and that we have a limited free will. The main desires are the same in all the creatures i.e. food, sex and territory. However the basic rule for all the creatures designed by the creator, they reckon, is the same as that of a hunter and the hunt policy. The animals' desires are controlled by nature, while the human desires are uncontrolled, thus a human has no limits to his desires, therefore it leads to the evils which has no limits. They reckon that if God had intended to establish peace in this world, there would have definitely been peace without fail. They said maybe that we are being penalised due to our own deeds, particularly our hatred against each other in the name of God, rather than to completely surrender to God and love all His creatures. They feel that the history is a witness that there has never been peace in this world and in view of the past history it is fair to say that it will continue like this or more likely get worse in view of the advancement of science and technology in the field of weapons of mass destruction.

One of the Children of God said, 'it is nothing but, Indoctrination.' He gave an example that, suppose, if Mr Alfa (Muslim), Mr Bravo (Jew) and Mr Charlie (Christian), were born and indoctrinated in opposite religions, they would have followed it accordingly, and might have been the champion of what they would have been brainwashed in and indoctrinated right from their childhood by their parents and their community. He said that these religions dictate others and claim that God belongs to them only, and it is their duty to protect God, whereas God is protector and provider to all His creatures. If they love God, or fear God, they should love all His creatures, not only if you join their camp. He said these religions are using the name of God for the recruitment of people into their camps as their Army, ready to fight in the name of God, each one claiming that God is on their side, which is a hard fact and a very sad part of their past history.

Life After Death - Heaven & Hell. Some of the Children of God do not believe in life after death and the heaven and hell concept, and they reckon that the human is born with different natural instincts to include kindness, passion, as well as evil which is a part of the creation of the human. Some of them said maybe that this world being very temporary and short stay is probably the heaven for some and hell for others, reasons best known to the creator. Whereas the world hereafter if any, is probably permanent, most beautiful, and a heaven for all, that no-one would like to come to this cruel, selfish and materialistic world, if given an option. All these religions claim that the only way to go to the heavens is if you join them otherwise you will end up in hell. Other religions are the same, who is right, and who is not? They said that, we do not mind if they feel good to go to the heavens, good luck to them, but why do they wish others to go to hell? It is simply a carrot and stick policy of a recruitment agency, according to their views.

Prophecies. Somehow, they got very much interested in the prophecies, which I explained as given under the headings, 'Prophecies about Jesus' and 'Prophecies about the Coming of Muhammad' (peace be upon both of them). Most of them said that, it is really amazing, but the prophecies had to be fulfilled so that the Scripture is completed, and the people were/are only the instruments to fulfil the prophecies. One person said, 'maybe that all humans are part of the Scripture which is being fulfilled as God desires.'

Adam & Eve. As regards Adam & Eve, some people reckon that it is more of fiction which does not appeal to their common sense, only the creator knows the truth. They reckon that since Adam was not created by his own choice, the fair option for him in the interest of his children was to request God to put him back to earth, so that his future generations are not put to test, deceived by Satan, and his children end up in hell hereafter. Does it make any sense at all that, we are being penalised due to the sin of Adam & Eve. Does it make any sense that Satan was created and allowed to mislead and misguide the people, if God intended peace and justice in this world. The Holy Books tell us that, the first murder of a human took place right under the nose of Adam, where his one son, Cain, killed his brother Abel. What an unfortunate start of the creature of human as per the fictions of these religions, according to this group. They said that even if we believe in this fiction that Satan is to deceive the human, then it is fair to say looking at the past history that, Satan has been extremely successful, particularly in deceiving the followers of these three religions of Judaism, Christianity and Islam, in killing each other, and killing among their own factions.

Some of the Children of God said that if science proves the story of Adam & Eve is wrong, then would these religions deny the science or their belief about Adam & Eve? Whereas, with faith, God will guide people to make their own law and path, and everything proved by science would simply be the will of God.

Darwin theory. Some people believe in Darwin theory, 'descent of man from Ape-like race.' I talked to some school children, who also think that we were the Ape-like race and have developed in to humans. The children are taught Darwin theory in schools and they also hear and learn from their parents, the church and the mosque, that we are the children of Adam & Eve. Let us therefore look as lay people at Darwin theory. During 1859 Darwin wrote a book 'Origin of Species', followed by another book 'Descent of Man from

Ape-like Race.' What effect did Darwin theory have during 19th century?

Darwin was a scientist and his theory was based upon his observations subject to some conditions to be fulfilled, because science had not developed at the time to prove it. This theory was misused by the evil people to justify their racial discrimination. History has witnessed the very sad events of racial discrimination and colonisation and the Second World War, before and after Darwin's theory, a few of which are mentioned below.

From the 16th century, the Europeans lacking God's consciousness started to colonise different parts of the world. Christopher Columbus led the first ever colonisation, where Spain invaded South America enslaving the simple native people who were living a peaceful life. The provinces of South America, rich in gold and silver were plundered by these invaders. Those who offered any resistance were brutally slaughtered. Afterwards the Spanish, the Portuguese, the Dutch, the French and the British took part in the competition of colonisation. Nineteenth century Britain became the world's greatest colonial empire from India to Latin America. The white man plundered the wealth of the innocent, weak and backward world by use of brutal force which they acquired through knowledge and technology.

Hitler, who was impressed with Darwin theory, was happy to believe the German to be a superior race to all other races. In order to establish the supremacy of the German race, Hitler started the Second World War, which ended in a disgraceful defeat of Germany and saw Hitler commit suicide.

Mussolini, the Italian dictator, was also impressed with Darwin theory. Italy occupied Ethiopia, considering them as an inferior race. The Nazi empire lost the war and Mussolini was executed by his own people.

In 1924, Joseph Stalin of Russia succeeded Lenin and was also impressed with Darwin theory. He introduced collectivism of land in Russia, where state land grains were harvested by armed troops. Hundreds of thousands who resisted his policies were sent to Siberia, and millions died as a result.

The Holy Books teach us that, all humans should be treated equally, kindly and justly, and not to cause mischief and corruption on the land. God loves those who are mindful of God and **race to do good**. It is therefore fair to say that, all humans are equal and brothers in humanity, if some need support and help, provide it, if not then, 'Live and Let Live.'

My Response to the Children of God. Having heard the various views from different people (male and female), which was much more challenging than I thought, I responded with a simple script that I had prepared beforehand as below:

It is good to know that you believe in one God, so to start with, we are not only brothers in humanity but brothers in faith of one God! 'That is right!' they said. I will provide you with the proof and evidence of the religions. I am sure you will agree with me that there is good and evil in our society? 'Yes of course!' These religions are meant to be mindful of God and do good There are three kinds of proof to include the miracles, the prophecies and of course the science. We cannot go back in time and witness the miracles ourselves, but I am sure you will agree with me that the people around at that time must have witnessed to believe what they believed. As regards the prophecies, they are amazing proof, for example, about the coming of Jesus and Muhammad (PBUT), hundreds of years before their birth, and about the future events, of which God alone could have had the knowledge. However, I will proceed with the proof of science, which you believe in. The Holy Qur'an is a book of signs, which leads the science in a direction to explore, and sure to find it to be true? 'We can't believe that!' I explained, as given under the headings of this book, 'The Holy Qur'an and Modern Science.' When asked how could it be possible that 1400 years ago, this knowledge could have arisen, the answer was nothing but, 'Absolutely amazing it is! Never heard of it! Continue!' If you read the Holy Qur'an, it confirms the previous revelations of the Torah, the Psalms, and the Gospels as the true revelations by God. It also confirms the previous Prophets Moses, David and Jesus as the Messengers of God and Muhammad (PBUT) as the last and final prophet with the last and final revelation of the Holy Qur'an. I will now explain to you about the common foundation of the revealed religions, where the previous revelations have revealed about the coming of Jesus and Muhammad (peace be upon both of them). There were miracles with God's permission blessed to the prophets, I explained, particularly the miraculous birth of Jesus (PBUH) without any male intervention, where he spoke as a child to defend his mother. You mentioned about the free will of humans with no limits to his desires as against the animals' desires, which are controlled. I sincerely believe that the religions are the best control of the human desires if he/she achieves God's consciousness, otherwise you are right that the human can be worse than animals.

You said that, 'I am not sure about the Last Day.' Let me tell you that, to believe in the Last Day is an integral part of our faith, besides believing in one God. The sole purpose of our life is to be mindful of God and do good deeds. The Last Day is a day of judgement, where we will all be held accountable for our deeds. He interrupted and said that, 'This is the only fiction I like the best, if it is so, many followers of these three religions will need sorting out.' In response, I said, there is a never ending list of very good things that these religions have done in the past, however they need to learn to differ, may God be kind to everyone, and we will only find out when we all return to God.

Another remark about the Prophet Abraham [PBUH]. Yes I agree with you that, a man of faith like Abraham will never ever discriminate between his wives and two small sons, and God has also been roped into it by some Jewish Scribes who have presented Sarah and Isaac superior to Hagar and Ishmael. I also agree with you that the Prophet Moses had shown his grave concern about the Scribes corrupting the Scripture, which was later confirmed by the Prophet Jeremiah. And you are right to say that the Qur'an has also revealed that the previous Scriptures are not preserved as revealed, and there are different factions in all these religions and also in Islam   However, I said that the factions are strictly forbidden in all these religions. While the Qur'an has revealed a severe warning not to divide into factions, it has also revealed that those who have divided into factions, do the righteous deeds, you will all return to God and he will make clear to you about your differences.

Another question. You asked if the laws of these religions are impractical/barbaric? You must understand that these religions are highly spiritual and the laws have been prescribed by the Lord who knows what is best about His creatures. These laws are harsh for the criminals only, and are meant to protect innocent people becoming the victims of lawless persons. As regards, 'if someone slaps you on one cheek, offer him the other as well, about Jesus' teachings,' it has a deep rooted psychology. It is the height of decency and humanity that he has focussed upon. If you offer the other cheek to a person, he/she will be hit hard by the shame and guilt, and will never do it again, which has an element of spirituality in the name of God. He/she who is the aggressor will and must be condemned by the society and even by his/her own parents, relatives and friends besides God. Does it make sense to you? 'It is the height of decency no doubt, but not practical,' he said. As regards the Muslim law to cut the hands of a thief, whether a man or a woman, I said that, first of all it is the responsibility of the Muslim state to ensure that everyone is provided with the opportunities to make an honest living. Those who are incapable of working, there is a provision for the state, as well as God fearing people who give charity so that the needy can survive respectfully. However, if some habitual thief wants to better his/her quality of life, and does not repent, then the law is harsh only on such criminals to protect the society. Does it make sense to you? 'I can see the point, but it is still a cruel desert law,' he said.

Another question from a couple (husband and wife). You asked that, these religions dictate others! Let me tell you about Islam. The Muslims are forbidden to argue, dictate, control or force anyone to convert into Islam. Instead they are commanded to show decent manners, use the best of their wisdom, knowledge and reasoning only to the extent of conveying the message that why we believe what we believe. It helps others to understand that Islam is a religion of peace and tolerance, and the Qur'an is a word of God, and a way of life for Muslims. However if someone embraces Islam at his/her own choice, he/she is most welcome. Does it answer your query? They said, 'It looks very good on the surface from all the three religions, but till such time you join their camp, they never treat you the same.'

Another question. You asked that 'the Jews, Christians and Muslims claim to go to heaven'! Let me first tell you that I wish all of them to go to heaven but it is absolute wishful thinking, it is the prerogative of God and God alone, as to who goes to the heavens. The Qur'an has repeatedly revealed about the Jews, Christians and the Muslims that those who are mindful of God and do good deeds have nothing to fear, they will not grieve. He interrupted me and said that, 'I am really amazed to know that the deeds are also the consideration in these three religions!' I continued and emphasised that, this is the real essence of these religions according to the Qur'an. I said that, God will judge us by our deeds, who knows our intentions? He asked me, 'What do you mean by deeds, is it to pray in a synagogue, church or mosque?' I replied that to pray to God is your personal bond with the God to worship Him, ask for help, blessings and guidance, and to achieve God's consciousness to do good deeds. The deeds are how to lead your way of life with honesty and high morals, and treat all humans with dignity and respect. He asked me, 'What about an oppressor, an oppressed, a corrupt, an honest, and a God fearing person who all offer their prayer in the same synagogue, church or mosque?' I replied that, the prayers of the people with evil deeds is nothing but a deceptive appearance, 'Façade', to deceive other people, but they cannot deceive God who knows the intentions and will judge them by their deeds. We must also judge others by their deeds, and not only by their duty of prayers. He said that, 'I am always mindful of God, I believe God is always with me, and it helps me to do good to all the humans most of the time, so I do not have to be the slave of the laws of any of the religions.'

Another remark by the Children of God was that the prophecies are the amazing proof, but it also means that, **'the people are only the instruments to fulfil the prophecies, maybe we are all part of the Scripture being fulfilled!'** I said that, it is a sign for the people to believe that, God alone has the knowledge of the future.

Last not the least, I explained to them my most favourite, Jesus teachings and the last Sermon of Prophet Muhammad (PBUT)

> **Jesus** [PBUH] **said, Golden Rule.** *"In everything do to others as you would have them do to you; for this is the law and the prophets."* ***(Matthew 7:12)***

Last Sermon of Prophet Muhammad [PBUH]. After praising and thanking God, (in brief), he said that, "hurt no one so that no one may hurt you. Remember you will indeed meet your Lord, and that **He will indeed reckon your deeds.** All mankind are from Adam and Eve, a white has no superiority over a black, nor a black has any superiority over white, **except by piety and good deeds**."

In response, most of them showed anger and said, 'What is the fuss these religions are making against each other, when each has been revealed a respective Holy Book from the same source to follow as they understand, and race to do good, like to compete for good deeds, and leave their

128

differences till they all return to God! We were of the opinion that these religions have failed their followers, but having heard you, we can say that their followers have failed the religions. However, we do not want to be part of the fighting force of any of these three religions whose elements have always caused mischief and corruption on the land, either among themselves or against each other.' They said that, 'We will rather worship God in our own ways, God is everywhere, not only in the synagogue, church or a mosque. We can worship God in our room on our own, eyes closed or open and focus on good deeds to the best of our honesty, love the animals, and have mutual respect for each other as brothers in humanity.' Some other people gave specific examples of three religions creating mischief and corruption on the land, assuring their followers that God is on their side. They said that Jesus' teachings are that, 'Whoever is not against us, is with us.' George Bush issued his own commandment that, 'either you are with us or against us.' And who was the biggest supporter of George Bush's policies? Tony Blair, another very good Christian. Look at the Iran-Iraq war, two Muslim countries killing each other claiming that God is on their side. Look at the world wars, the Christians killing each other, each claiming that God is on their side, look at the Jews committing atrocities against the Palestinian Muslims (their cousin brothers), and that they all claim to be the champions of peace,' were their views.

I asked them, though you do not want to join any religion, can you tell me the reasons which convinced you that these religions are the true religions? The answer was, 'The Qur'an, the fulfilment of prophecies about Jesus, and God spoke direct to Moses.' They said that the prophecies and their fulfilment (despite different interpretations) are the proof that these are revealed Holy Books. The Qur'an is an amazing Book (the mother of all sciences), definitely the word of God. I corrected them that, the Qur'an is not a Book of Science, but a Book of signs for all times. They said that, it is good to know that the Qur'an confirms the previous Holy Books, and encourages them to follow their own religions with a common faith in God, and the common purpose, 'to be mindful of God and do good deeds.' They said that, 'Jesus teachings and the last Sermon of your Prophet really touched our hearts, because it shows regards for the whole of humanity.' They said that if God spoke direct to Moses, then we can imagine why Jews believe what they believe. They also said that the fulfilment of the prophecies about Jesus according to the Christians, are mind blowing, and we can imagine, 'why Christians believe what they believe.' The Qur'an is word of God, and we now understand, why Muslims believe what they believe. They said that, the solution about the differences in the Qur'an is the only solution, 'race to do good,' you will all return to God and He will make clear to you the matters you used to dispute about.' We thank you for sharing the knowledge, and from now on, we will definitely have much more respect for all these three religions, however we will respect their followers provided they show regards for the whole of humanity, race to do good and leave their differences till they all return to God, they said.

I closed the dialogue with my remarks that, it is a never ending list of very good things that the followers of these religions have done in the past, however they need to learn to differ, and work together to establish peace and justice for all in our world. It was a hard task, I could not do any more, however I critically analysed what they said. My analysis is that they are mindful of God, and sincerely do good deeds. Probably they might have been the part of a religion, but they are thoroughly put off by the uncalled behaviour of some of the followers of these three religions, which is a lesson to be learnt by all concerned.

Note. My parents used to tell me, and I tell the same to my children, that there are two things in life that you must take positively, because it helps you to be on the right track: 'Friends advise and taunt by others.' There is one very important taunt of all the taunts by the children of God to the followers of the religions of Holy Books mentioned above. I never thought about it, till I was hit so hard by this taunt, that I had no good answer. I will come to it later in my book to explain it, which can be extremely useful to keep us on the right track. *Question to the Readers:* Which one you thinks is the most important taunt of all the taunts by the children of God, to the people of revealed Books, that they can benefit from?

A Trial to Proclaim to the Christians (Four Step Guide)

Step 1. 'Our Nearest Friends are Christians,' Reveals the Holy Qur'an. To start with, you will be glad to know that Islam is the only Non Christian faith, which has in its article of faith that 'No Muslim is a Muslim, unless he believes in Jesus Christ (PBUH).' Muhammad (PBUH) is mentioned only five times in the Qur'an, while Jesus is mentioned 25 times, and there is a separate Sura 19, in honour of Mary, the mother of Jesus. The life of Muslims as you know, revolves around the Qur'an, and let me read to you a few verses from the Qur'an, about the special status of Jesus (PBUH), the Gospels and the Christians.

Mary is preferred by God over all the women of the world.

'The angel said to Mary: "Mary, God has chosen you, purified you, and preferred you over all the women of the world."' *(Qur'an 3:42)*

'Mary said, "How can I bear a son when no man has touched me, nor I have been unchaste?", and Gabriel said, "your Lord said, 'It is easy for me, **We shall make him a sign to all people, a mercy from Us.** When He decrees something, He says only, 'Be', and it becomes at once."' *(Qur'an 19:20-21,35)*

'When God will say, "Jesus, son of Mary! Remember My favour to you and your mother, how I **strengthened you with the Holy Spirit**, when you spoke to people as an infant and at the age of maturity." *(Qur'an 5:110)*

'Recall, when God said, "Jesus, I will take you back and raise you up to Me. I will purify you of the disbelievers, and till the Day of Resurrection**, I will make those who follow you superior to those who disbelieved you**."' *(Qur'an 3:55)*

'We sent after them Jesus, son of Mary, confirming the Torah which had been sent before. We gave him the Gospel with **guidance and light.** So let the follower of the Gospel judge according to God has sent down in it. And those who do not judge by what God has sent down are lawbreakers.' *(Qur'an 5:46,47)*

The second coming of Jesus (PBUH). The Qur'an confirms the second coming of Jesus.

'Surely Jesus is a sign of the Hour' **(Qur'an 43:61).** *'There is not any one of the People of Book who will not believe in Jesus before his death, and on the Day of Resurrection he will be a witness against them'* **(Qur'an 4:159).**

*'We have prescribed a law and a path to each of you. If God had so willed, He would have made you all one community, but He desired to test you in different ways through that which He has given to you, **so race to do good:** you will all return to God and He will make clear to you the matters you used to dispute about.'* **(Qur'an 5:48)**

Have you understood, I asked? They replied: 'What a beautiful message that, we will be tested in different ways! It is an honour for Mary, Jesus and the Christianity, though differently! I like about the Holy Spirit of Jesus! I like that you believe in the miraculous birth of Jesus and his miracles though differently! It is good to know that you believe in Jesus as a messiah, raised by God to Himself and in his second coming though differently!'
Let me read a few more verses of the Holy Qur'an:

*'Surely for Muslims, Jews and the Christians, whosoever believes in God and the Last Day and do **good deeds**, shall have nothing to fear, nor shall they grieve.'* **(Qur'an 5:69)**

*'Whichever direction you turn to pray, **'race to do good'**, and wherever you might be, God will bring you all together.'* **(Qur'an 21:49)**

What do you understand about God will bring us together, I asked? 'Well it can only be in the heavens or hell! I managed not to laugh and said that, it means to believe in the God of Moses, do good deeds and whichever direction we turn to pray, He will bring us together in the heavens. He said, We believe in our Holy Bible as the true message of God of Moses, and surely God will reward us for our good deeds. I pray and wish God's blessings for the Muslims as well as others. The final decision lies with God alone, who revealed the messages and the final results we will find out when we all return to God. Meanwhile let us together serve the humanity which will bring us together in the heavens

And finally listen to this, I read:

> *'You are sure to find of all the people, the nearest in friendship to the Muslims are those, who say, 'We are Christians', because there are people among them who are open to learning and practice strict self discipline.'*
> ***(Qur'an 5:82,83)***

What are your sincere feelings about it, I asked? Various responses: 'Beautiful, shake hand, we are friends! That is very nice, at least we are not enemies! Let us be friends! It is a great honour for the Christians! It is all about good deeds! Why don't you become a Christian and we will be best friends?' We laughed, and I said, it is a good question and I will definitely come to it later! A good friend of mine said, 'It took you 1400 years to know that we are your friends?' I responded, excuse me mate, do I look 1400 years old like you? He laughed. I said your ancestors, generations after generations were hammered by the Jews and the Romans and in turn, you have been taking it out on us, because we are not good politicians. Unlike Jews, we Muslims love Jesus in our own ways, we keep reminding you that we are not your enemies, but your nearest friends. He replied, 'No I was joking, all of us have been crazy, Islam is a very good religion of your choice. It is high time we became friends and work together for peace and justice,' and we laughed.

About another question from a lady, 'Why your Muslims say that, 'islam is the only religion accepted to God, when according to your Holy Qur'an 'if God had so willed He would have made you all one community but He desired to test you in different ways through that which He has given you'? I clarified it before proceeding any further that, the word islam means. 'complete devotion/ submission to God', which is the faith, whereas the religion Islam means faith combined with the law and path for the Muslims revealed in the Qur'an. The Jews, Christians and Muslims are supposed to have a common faith but each has been prescribed a different law and path in their respective Holy Books as revealed in the Qur'an. Hope it answers your query? Got it! It is so crucial to understand the context rather than a text! They all do it to mislead others or through ignorance, be it Jews, Christians or Muslims!

Step 2. Islam is a Religion of Peace and Tolerance. Let me start with the last Sermon of our Prophet Muhammad (PBUH). After praising and thanking God (a very small brief below), he said:

> *"Hurt no one so that no one may hurt you. Remember you will indeed meet your Lord, and that He will indeed reckon your deeds. All mankind are from Adam and Eve, a white has no superiority over a black, nor a black has any superiority over white, except by **piety and good deeds**."*

You must have heard the common word of Jihad, associated with the Muslims? 'Yes,' they replied. You will be surprised to know that there is no word Jihad in the Qur'an, and I do not need to elaborate on it any more. However, there is a word Jahada, which means struggle and strive against the evils of oneself and the society. I will read one or two verses of the Qur'an about the central message of the religion of Islam about peace even during the war, fighting back the aggressor and combating terrorism. I read the Qur'an 5:32, 'Killing any innocent person, regardless of religion, race or colour is a very major sin in Islam.' I read other verses that Muslims are strictly forbidden to be aggressors, but only to fight back the aggressors and to help those who call for help to fight the aggressor. Never to be the aggressor also means never to use aggressive language to hurt other religions/communities. Self defence however, does not mean that we are not allowed to attack, but it means that we should not be the first to be aggressors or the cause of aggression. In case we are attacked, we are allowed to attack back the way we were attacked. Even while fighting back the aggressor, there are so many strings attached to it, in terms of restrictions and prohibitions that if the enemy stops, you must stop, do not exceed the limits, killing innocent civilians is prohibited, instead protect those not involved in fighting, because peace is always preferred over the war.

As regards terrorism, I read the relevant verses given above under the heading 'Guidelines about Combating Terrorism in the Qur'an,' that Islam considers terrorism worse than killing and we must combat terrorism till it is totally eliminated. However Islam instructs to address the root causes of terrorism in the first place, which is injustice, victimisation, lack of awareness and discrimination. Unfortunately there is state terrorism, individuals and organisations of Muslims and Non Muslims who are involved in terrorist activities. I asked them, can you think of a better version of peace than this? 'It is a very peaceful guideline! We cannot blame the religion Islam! I wish they act upon it! State terrorism is the worst! It is the politicians responsible for wars!' These were the responses from the Christians.

One common question was, 'Why do all the terrorists happen to be Muslims?' I will definitely come to it a little later, I said.

Step 3. The Qur'an is Word of God. I will explain to you, the very foundation of these three religions from your Bible **(Genesis, 21:12,13).** I went through the prophecies about the coming of Muhammad (PBUH), and I explained as given under the heading 'Background History of the Revealed Religions' in this book. Having read the text of the Bible that God will raise a prophet from the children of Hagar, because they are also the offspring of Abraham, I asked, do you agree with this statement in the Bible? 'Yes, of course,' he said, 'if the Bible says so then your Prophet Muhammad must be a Prophet of God. Basically we are both looking up to one and the same God in the heaven, and His commandments through our Holy Books as we understand it, and the purpose of our life is to worship God and be good to each other. Can you tell me about the crucifixion of Jesus (PBUH) in the Qur'an?' Very important question, I will definitely come to it later, I said.

Let us have a look at the proof that, the Qur'an is a word of God. There are three types of proof that we can provide, the miracles, prophecies and the science. We cannot go back in time to verify the miracles, however I will explain only one miracle about Jesus' birth given in the Qur'an. Do you agree with the science, I asked? 'Yes! The Qur'an is the only Holy

Book which can be proven by modern science,' was the response. I explained as given under the heading of 'the Qur'an and Modern Science.' I asked, who could have had such knowledge about science, 1400 years ago, any man on our planet or God alone, the Lord of our world, the lord of universe? 'We have never known anything like this!' they said. 'It is simply amazing! Can't deny it! I will study the Qur'an more thoroughly! This is a miracle! Apparently it makes sense, but I do not have enough knowledge, so better follow my church! It is too complicated! Too much to handle in this world, bills, job, above all my girl friend and have no time to dig the details.' Some people said, 'the Qur'an is good but we see Islam through Muslim countries where there is no justice for a common man, the different factions are always at each other throat, and the animals are not treated kindly. There are hardly any human rights in the Muslim countries. We are not blaming the community because most of them are the victims'. I said that, it is mainly due to the ruling class and their supporters who are in control of their affairs. They believe in God but neither they love nor fear God, to ensure peace, justice and equality of human rights because the ruling class do not follow the essence of the Qur'an. Most of the Muslims are God fearing people but they are helpless, however I will come back to it later.

Let me now explain to you about Jesus ^(PBUH)' birth as given in the Qur'an, which I did as given under the heading of 'Jesus and Mary in the Qur'an.' I asked them about their feelings. 'Really touched my heart! With this miracle, Mary's family and the people around would have definitely believed her about the fulfilment of the prophecy about the miraculous birth of the child Jesus! The amazing miracle but why is it not in Gospels? It was the fulfilment of the prophecy about

Jesus' birth.' These were the different responses with definite emotions, as revealed in the Holy Qur'an!

I said that, we Muslims have exactly the same faith of Abraham, Moses and of Jesus, which Jesus (PBUT) answered to a Jew's question, 'Which one is the most important commandment?' It is given in your Holy Bible, I said, and can you please read it for me, also about whom to worship in your prayers as per Jesus teachings.

> 'Jesus answered, "The first is, 'Hear, O Israel: the Lord our God, the Lord is one; you shall love the Lord your God with all your heart, and with all your soul, and with all your mind, and with all your strength."' **(Mark 12:28-30)**

> 'But whenever you pray, go into your room and shut the door and pray to your Father who is in secret; and your Father who sees in secret will reward you.' **(Matthew 6:6)**

I thanked him for reading the Holy Bible for me, and asked him, whom do you think Jesus is saying to pray to and He will reward? 'The Father in secret,' he replied. I said, you are absolutely right, because Jesus himself was not in secret when he said so, it was about none but, 'God alone,' that we worship. There is not a single unequivocal statement where Jesus (PBUH) himself said that, 'I am God and worship me', and that there is no word trinity in the Holy Bible. I then reminded them about our common terms, 'believe in one God, associate no partners with Him and worship none but Him alone.' In reply they said that, 'It is not about the word trinity in the Holy Bible, it is about the essence of the fulfilment of all the prophecies about Jesus, and what Jesus finally said after his resurrection, 'Go therefore and make disciples of all nations, baptizing them in the name of the

Father and of the Son and of the Holy Spirit', (Matthew 28:19). No one on earth has seen the Father. The son from the heaven has seen Him and bears witness of Him, doing His works and speaking His words. Therefore we believe in one God, associate no partners with Him, and worship none but Him alone with His three characteristics, God the Father, the Son and the Holy Spirit.' I asked them about the Holy Spirit. They said, 'If we are mindful of God the Father, the Son and the Holy Spirit, we are guided by the Holy Spirit which means God is with us.' I asked, how do you know that you are guided by the Holy Spirit? 'It inspires us to love and help all the humans regardless of their belief, love all other creatures of God, and love His environment, and make our life and the life of others cheerful, full of fun and excitement. If we do evil deeds as a way of life, Jesus will be hurt, we confess, as well as repent, and we hope for forgiveness through Jesus [PBUH]

I said to them that the Holy Qur'an has revealed that, 'Jesus [PBUH] was not God, but a Messenger of God, who gave life to the dead and performed other miracles with God's permission. And God can do anything what He intends to do. When He decrees something, He says only, 'Be,' and it becomes at once. It is also revealed that some of the records in the Bible are not preserves as revealed.' They said that, 'You are absolutely right. No human but only God can give life to a dead human, so did Jesus with the will of his Father in heaven to fulfil the prophecy. No human can be born of a virgin mother, no human can foretell about the exact details as to how he will be betrayed by one of his disciples, delivered in the hands of evildoers and crucified, will be resurrected on the third day and raised to the heavens by his Father. Jesus foretold about these things, and also these were the prophecies fulfilled, and witnessed

140

by people of the time. We are certain like death that, God can do anything what He intends to do, and God is entitled to have His three characteristics, God the Father, the Son and the Holy Spirit. According to the prophecies, God intended to visit our world in human form, it was not a surprise visit, but a deliberately planned visit revealed in the prophecies, which was fulfilled through Jesus. Jesus was telling them that, no human including him in human form can do such things but with the will of his Father in heaven, which are the characteristics of one and the same God.' They said that, 'We know you want us to convert to Islam, and we take it as a big favour of yours, because it is a test of our faith in Jesus, and certainly we will pass the test, and may God reward you for that, because you are doing your duty.' They got emotional about the records of the Bible not preserved as revealed and said that, 'We Christians have become a sandwich in between the Hebrew Bible and the Qur'an. Our Gospels besides Jesus' teachings are mainly an account of the fulfilment of the prophecies in the Hebrew Bible about Jesus. Records or no records, our belief is based upon the fulfilment of the prophecies, which were the physical acts witnessed by the people of the time. After about 600 years of Jesus, according to your Qur'an, divinity, trinity, Jesus son of God, crucifixion, resurrection of Jesus are all denied. Neither it changes the prophecies about Jesus nor their fulfilment through Jesus. However, we must say that, your Holy Qur'an has given a beautiful solution which has impressed us the most, 'race to do good, you will all return to God and He will make clear to you the matters you used to dispute about.' They went on, 'We will be tested through our Holy Bible as we understand it, while you will be tested through your Holy Qur'an as you understand it, therefore we both must follow our respective law and path, and not get into a blame game as advised in your Holy

Qur'an. There is no other alternative but to wait till the second coming of Jesus (PBUH), that we both believe in, and then he will make clear to us about the differences, meanwhile let us be cheerful and serve the humanity.'

One lady said, 'Your Holy Qur'an is an amazing Book, which we all need to understand it with an open mind and in the overall context of the Holy Bible. As I understand it from your Holy Qur'an, we are all being tested in different ways through our respective revealed Scriptures and each of us must sincerely follow our own Holy Book as we understand it. Indeed it strengthens my believe in Jesus to know that, no Muslim can be a Muslim unless he/she believes in Jesus Christ despite it is different to us according to your Holy Qur'an. As a mother, while I groom my children to believe in Jesus (PBUH), I also make sure that my children do not blame any other child or person for their belief, but to love and respect them to please Jesus (PBUH). However, I will have to explain to my children particularly about our spiritual differences with Islam with a view to understand and respect each other. I am sure that the Muslim mothers would also groom their children to follow their beautiful religion Islam, and have mutual respect for all others regardless of any religion. Surely our arguments and the attitudes of dictating and blaming each other will not please God, but as per your Holy Qur'an, 'race to do good, you will all return to God and He will make clear to you the matters you used to dispute about', will definitely please God'.

I responded to the questions I promised to come to later, namely Sunni's, Shia's and others fighting each other, and who is right and who is wrong. I said, before I reply to you, can I ask you about Catholics, Protestants, Orthodox, and others, who is right and who is wrong? 'They all cannot be right,' he said. I had the appropriate verses of the Qur'an 3:103,105, and 6:159 flagged and I asked him to please read as given above, 'About Factions.' I thanked him for reading. It is self explanatory that to split into factions is forbidden both in Islam as well as Christianity. I reminded him the past history about the Catholics versus Protestants versus Orthodox and so on, despite clear instructions in the Bible not to divide into factions. There is no name of any faction mentioned in the Qur'an, however Sunni's and Shia's are also wrong to split into factions and very wrong to fight against each other. To my understanding, there must not be factions, they are all Muslims but if they have divided into factions, as long as they are mindful of God and do good deeds, there should not be hatred towards each other. But when the factions are politically motivated, some of the Misguided Religious Leaders are highly professional to invoke hatred among their innocent followers. Again the solution is to bring the awareness to the public who should condemn such leaders who invoke hatred against each other, and to be mindful of God, race to do good and leave the differences till we all return to God.

Another question, 'the Qur'an is good but we see Islam through Muslim countries, where there is no justice for a common man who is subjected to suppression, corruption, no human rights and the animals are not treated with kindly. He said, I am not blaming the whole community because most of them are victims or helpless, I am talking about the governments in the Muslim countries'. I did not have a very good answer to this question about the facts on the ground, however I picked up some courage and said, it is sad, but may I remind you about the history of Great Britain before the enlightenment, where the common man was enslaved to the church and the kings. I am pleased that, you people have come out of it, and may be one day we can also come out of it, provided our young generation learns the essence of the Qur'an, which is to, 'be mindful of God and do good deeds,' which ensures protection, opportunities and justice for all. However, I can proudly say that, our world witnessed the very first time a practical demonstration of justice, equality of humans dignity, protection of weak, helpless, and rights for women during the time of our Prophet, and the rightly guided Caliphs. We agreed that, together we can proclaim and support the suppressed people against the suppressors, regardless of their religions.

Another question, 'Why do all the terrorists happen to be Muslims?' The history is a witness that the state of Israel came into being as a result of a terrorist movement. History is also full of examples where Christians have been involved not only as individuals and small organisations, but also through state terrorism. Whosoever is therefore involved directly or indirectly in terrorist activities is committing a grave sin and must be stopped at all costs, be it any religion, individual, any organisation or a state. Islam preaches to combat terrorism, and in the first instance tackles the root cause of the terrorism, which is injustice, discrimination and victimisation, and lack of awareness. We do not want to get into a blame game, but you tell me your honest feelings and impression about the message of Islam that I explained to you? 'You are right, the Qur'an is totally against terrorism,' he replied.

Another question. You asked me about the crucifixion of Jesus in the Qur'an. The Qur'an says, 'They neither killed him, nor crucified him, **it was made to appear like that to them,** he was taken up by God to Himself.' They asked me to read this verse again, which I did. They said that, 'We are both right according to the Qur'an. The people around that time believed what was made to appear like that to them, and you are right to believe what was revealed to you 600 years after Jesus. The people did not witness Jesus being raised by God to Himself at the time of Crucifixion, but they did witness Jesus being raised by God to Himself after the resurrection, and it was mainly a prophecy about Jesus, hundreds of years before the birth of Jesus which was fulfilled.' In reply I said, Jesus must have been replaced by another man to be on the Cross and raised by God to Himself at the will of God. 'The crucifixion, the Cross, and resurrection are central to our belief of the fulfilment of the prophecies about Jesus. The body of Jesus was placed in the Tomb in the presence of so many witnesses, the body was guarded by the soldiers, resurrection of Jesus was witnessed by the disciples and many others. It may be that God wanted us to be a different community from the Jews and Muslims, what matters is good deeds,' he said. 'Before I thank you for sharing the knowledge,' he continued, 'I must say that the last Sermon of your Prophet really touched my heart, he must be a man of peace, with due regards for the whole humanity, may God bless his soul in peace. I along with my Christian and Muslim friends would love to proclaim this message of Muhammad and Jesus' (PBUT) teachings.'

Another pending question. You asked me, why don't I become a Christian, and we can be best friends? I said. you are missing the point that Judaism, Christianity and Islam as per the Holy Qur'an are the revealed religions of God. They are supposed to have a common faith of Abraham and Moses (complete devotion to God), but they have been prescribed a different law and path as per their revealed Books. The real challenge for us is to be the best friends as Christians and Muslims, because the essence of our religions is the same, 'be mindful of God and do good deeds,' and together we can work towards a greater cause of Jesus and Muhammad [PBUT] for helping the poor and helpless of our world. Like we Muslims believe in the Holy Bible and follow our own religion, you may also believe in Prophet Muhammad and the Holy Qur'an, with the common faith of Abraham, and follow your own religion? 'We can either believe in one or the other,' he said. **'To believe in the Qur'an means to disbelieve in the fulfilment of the prophecies about Jesus [PBUH]**, which were physical acts witnessed by the people of the time. And we have always regarded Abraham as our father in faith (complete devotion to God), even before your Qur'an. Indeed the prophecies about God visiting our world in human form were revealed and fulfilled through Jesus after the life of Abraham. However, I have understood the message, and I have been highly impressed with the noble teachings of the Holy Qur'an, but I am comfortable with my Holy Bible. I offer my whole hearted support to work together, to follow the mission of Jesus and Muhammad [PBUT] to reach to the poor, helpless and victims. Before I thank you for sharing your knowledge with me, I must say that, I do love the verse of your Qur'an, **'race to do good.'** You will all return to God and He will make clear to you the matters you used to dispute about.'

Most of the people were touched by the verses of the Holy Qur'an, they asked many questions and I finished with the miraculous birth of Jesus in the Qur'an. When I finished, I asked them, 'Do you think, we are your enemies?' It was good to find a mixed response from them and also the views of many other Christians about the Muslims:

'Not at all! I have so many Muslim friends.[1]
They are different but very nice people! The Muslims are
very hospitable. We need to follow some of their culture![2]
The young Muslims are lovely, full of humour, good laugh.[3]
The Muslims are in minority. It is our duty to care for them.[4]
They are well meaning, I love their curry![5]
We must respect every religion and their practice.[6]
This is their country, the young generation will surely work it
out, what is best for their own country.[7]
Some Muslims like to dictate their religion to us![8]
Some Muslim extremists hate us due to our religion, is it the
teaching in your religion?[9]
The Muslims should cheer up, life comes once only!'[10]

I responded to one remark that, 'some Muslims hate us due
to our religion!' I said that, I must apologise on their behalf
and assure you that, no Muslim who has a basic knowledge
of the Holy Qur'an will ever hate anyone due to his/her
religion or no religion. The Holy Qur'an tells us that, the
source of the revelation of the Holy Bible is the same God,
the Lord of the universe who has also revealed the Holy
Qur'an. Islam therefore teaches Muslims about an
honourable status particularly for the People of Book.
However there are some misguided people in both the
religions who need to get back to the basics of the Holy
Bible and the Holy Qur'an for guidance. He was satisfied
and said, 'Never mind, life goes on.'

Step 4. Let us Race to do Good. Let us be frank that
there are similarities and differences between the Christians
and the Muslims. The best option is, try to understand each
other's point of view and finally learn to differ, we will all
return to God and He will make clear to us, the matters we
used to dispute about, as revealed in the Holy Qur'an. I

pointed out that being mindful of God, with good deeds, if God Almighty so wishes, we may find a Jew, a Christian and a Muslim standing shoulder to shoulder next to each other in the heavens, regretting, why did we not stand shoulder to shoulder with each other during the short span of life we had? A bit too late, isn't it? Very well said. Hope everybody thinks like that.

At this stage I reminded them about the verse of the Holy Qur'an, 'you are sure to find of all the people the nearest in friendship to the Muslims are those who say, 'we are Christians.' Both the religions are blessed with the Holy Books from the same source, the Lord of the universe. Both the religions believe in the second coming of Jesus. I said, maybe God has blessed the Christians and Muslims with the responsibility to work together to establish peace and justice for all before the second coming of Jesus. I asked them, do you remember the verse of the Qur'an about Mary, the mother of Jesus? 'Yes, we do, "God has preferred Mary over all the women of the world."' They said. I said, I would not hesitate at all to say that, Mary is the mother of the Christians and the Muslims. Maybe, our mother Mary has got some blessings for us, and also a stick in her hand like an angry mother, telling us, "Stop behaving like kids. Get out now. Go and work together to help those in need and in pain before Jesus comes." I can definitely see a stick in her hand, but I am not sure about her good wishes for her children, but not all the children are alike, and after all mother is a mother. That is how I interpret the above verse of the Qur'an about the friendship of Christians and Muslims in the larger interest for all in our world, particularly for Non Christians and Non Muslims. They started clapping, and said, 'Well said mate, we need both, the blessings but definitely a stick.' I said, do you think that, we can work together to promote peace and justice, protect the animals from cruelty, reach the poor, helpless, in pain and victims, and be a role model to the world? 'Definitely! Sure! 100%! Very good! Let us plan and do it! Very noble cause, I would love to be involved! Shake hand, together we will do it! We have no time (jobs, bills to pay, and children to look after) but we must find time to protect cruelty to animals,' a couple (husband and wife) said. These responses reminded me exactly what the Qur'an has revealed about their emotions. Many of them asked me, 'Why don't I write a book and we will proclaim this message to our Christian friends and family, as well as to our Muslim friends, because it is a beautiful message, it is all about peace, have a laugh together and do good for others, the whole humanity.' I was touched the most by a simple response from a couple (husband and wife) who said that, 'they had no time (jobs, bills to pay, and children to look after), but they must find time to protect cruelty to animals.' I asked them why do you people love animals so much? 'The animals cannot express themselves,' they replied, 'they do not vote for any political party, they are in our control, we benefit so much from the animals, it is our duty and it is a nice feeling to love the animals and protect them. In reply, I said, 'Sure shot, God will bless you my friends in this world and the world hereafter, are my sincere wishes.'

It is fair to conclude that we should not at all be surprised if the Christians also use my book to proclaim, and it becomes a two-way traffic of friendship. I wished my book was complete, which is specific to the subject, short and easy to understand, which I could have given them as a present.

A Trial to Proclaim, the Views of Some Muslims

The life of Muslims revolves around the Holy Qur'an. Arabic may not be their first language, but they can read and recite the Qur'an. After my successful trial with the Christians, I decided to share my knowledge with the Muslims, particularly the young male and female Muslims of Great Britain. I started with the verse of the Qur'an, 'You are sure to find that the nearest in friendship to Muslims are those who say, 'We are Christians.' I explained it as given under the headings, 'Our Nearest Friends are Christians, Reveals the Holy Qur'an'. As expected, I was impressed with their positive response, because our Muslims are God fearing people, keen to know the true message of God, and they will render unquestioning obedience to that. I explained to them that I intend to write a book about 'Race to do Good,' to provide the knowledge and information of the Holy Books, to proclaim to integrate, and to integrate to proclaim, and work together to promote peace and justice. I did not have to do any further explanation, because only one verse of the Qur'an 5:48 already mentioned sums up the context of the whole message. I explained to them that this is not to prove them wrong, but with a view to understand each other, race to do good, and in the process to remind them about our common terms. It was good to clarify that there is no compulsion in the religion, we must not dictate, control, or blackmail anyone to convert to Islam. I reminded them that depending upon our good deeds and being mindful of God, if God Almighty so wishes, we may find a Jew, a Christian and a Muslim standing shoulder to shoulder in the heavens, only to regret that, why did we not stand shoulder to shoulder during that short span of life we had? A bit too late, isn't it? A very good response from each and every Muslim I spoke to and they assured me of their full support for this noble cause.

It was good to know their mixed feelings and also the views of many other Muslims about Christians as given below:

Both the communities love Jesus *(PBUH)*, *though in their own ways, but love is love.[1]*
Mary is mother to us, as well as to the Christians! I hope we do not start fighting like kids that, Mary is my mum'![2]
They believe in trinity, and will not be able to enter paradise.[3]
'Only one sect of Muslims will enter paradise, 72 sects will go to hell', a common known Hadith. What matters is the righteous deeds for the followers of the Holy Books.[4]
Every mother brings up her child to have God's blessings for this life and the life hereafter. God will decide as He wishes.[5]
Those who seek guidance from the Holy Books as they understand it, their case rests with the source of the message (God alone) who has revealed the Holy Books. What matters is their righteous deeds.[6]
We must respect them as the followers of the Holy Book, revealed by the same source to a different community as God had so willed and revealed in the Holy Qur'an.[7]
The Christians have anti-Muslim policies![8]
We have been prescribed a different law and path, so we should not be nosy to criticise others, but to follow ours.[9]
We should prove by our deeds that we are good Muslims.[10]
They are lovely people, but when they are drunk, most of them are a good laugh, while some become violent![11]
It is good to be friends and work together for a noble cause.[12]

We must stop the 'misguided Muslims', who invoke hatred against other communities or among the various factions, and the Christians should also do the same.[13]

The Christians are animal loving, charitable, kind hearted to accommodate all communities, and religions which is commendable. Surely God will reward them![14]

We must render unquestioning obedience to the commandment of God, and treat them as our nearest friends, and leave the differences till we all return to God.[15]

Except very few, most of Christians, are very peaceful people![16]

Except very few, most of Muslims are very peaceful people. With our attitudes we can improve things or make it worse![17]

Non Arab Muslims are treated as third class citizens by our so called Muslim brothers. While in Great Britain, we Muslims have equal rights as British citizens![18]

There is no compulsion in the religion, and we can convey the message, only if we have the decency to be friends.[19]

Some of the religious leaders of both the communities are mainly responsible in 'pulling us apart'.[20]

The differences among the factions of each community are even worse and frustrating. They do not even pray in the same church or mosque![21]

The Holy Bible and the Holy Qur'an are both messages of peace and justice for the whole of humanity. We should understand them.[22]

Let us open a centre in the UK to integrate to, 'race to do good', for the benefit of our future generations.[23]

I am sorry to say that, your book is wishful thinking, a weird dream and waste of time and energy. The Christians and Muslims, with their dedicated factions, get a kick and excitement out of sending each other to hell to please their ego, while you are dreaming about them working together to serve the humanity to please God. They will rather prefer to

152

be in their ghettoes to cling on to their communities. Let Jesus (PBUH) *sort out this mess in his second coming, and don't waste your time. However, I would love to join you, just to keep reminding you that it can never work!*[24]

All the Muslims agreed with me that, no doubt, Great Britain is second to none compared to the rest of the world of today, 'to allow to preach and practice one's religion, to provide protection (person, property and dignity), opportunities, and justice for all.' Let us work together to follow the footsteps of the struggle of Jesus and Muhammad (peace be upon them) in support of victims, and protect animals from cruelty.

I was already encouraged by the Christians I spoke to during the trial. The Muslims also assured me they would join this noble cause, except for one person who is willing to join but he reckons that, it can never work. I have however produced this book hoping that at least it will prove useful for the Christians and Muslims to understand each other, and help a dialogue between the two

Note. Earlier, I asked you a question about the most important taunt to the people of Holy Books from the Children of God, which can be to our benefit? Let us find the answer, see if you got it right!

On the Day When God assembles all the Messengers

Only God alone, knows what will happen, but let us carry out an imaginary exercise about, 'On the Day, when God assembles All the Messengers,' to enquire about the grandchildren of Abraham (PBUH). Let us find out, I am sure that, God will definitely have the answer.

God first summoned Abraham (PBUH), to explain the uncalled behaviour of many of his grandchildren, who are responsible for causing mischief and corruption on His land.

Abraham (PBUH) of course had a meeting with Moses, Jesus and Muhammad in the heavens, to discuss and prepare himself to explain before the Court of Lord. I wonder, how proud Abraham would be, and how proud Moses, Jesus and Muhammad would be during this meeting because of the behaviour of their followers. And the meeting starts (peace be upon all of them)!

Abraham (PBUH) started crying and said, 'God has summoned me to explain about the uncalled behaviour of many of my grandchildren, who are causing mischief and corruption on His land. What do you want me to say to the Lord?' Great wisdom in reply from all of them as expected. They also started crying, and continued crying, and wisely or embarrassingly did not utter a single word, till the meeting was over.

Abraham (PBUH) was on his way to the Court of Lord, and someone from behind tapped on his shoulder, so he stopped. He said to Abraham ^(PBUH), 'Sir, Moses, Jesus and Muhammad were only to deliver the message, which they did to the peril of their life. Abraham ^(PBUH) burst into anger and said, 'I have been summoned by the Lord, not about the delivery of the message, but the execution of message which has been deliberately disobeyed by many of my grandchildren.' He said, 'Sir believe me, many of your grandchildren are really wonderful and have been extremely useful and obedient in my experience. If you want I can come with you to the Court of Lord, as a witness to their best behaviour.' Abraham ^(PBUH) turned back abruptly, when he saw someone running away, '**Satan, the devil.**'

Abraham ^(PBUH) appeared before the Court of Lord, had nothing to say and continued crying. God also started crying and said, 'What to do with this lot, I revealed to them a simple solution':

Qur'an 5:48. 'We have prescribed a law and path to each of you. If God had so willed, He would have made you all one community, but He desired to test you in different ways through that which He has given you. So **'race to do good.'** You will all return to God, and He will make clear to you the matters you used to dispute about.'

The Higher You Go, The Harder You Fall.

The Jews, Christians and Muslims have been given the divine knowledge through the Holy Books, and they may not qualify for the benefit of doubt as against those who do not have the knowledge. It will be wishful thinking for those who think that they are given the Holy Books, and that they will not be tested for their deeds. While there is a very high reward for the righteous deeds in the name of God for the blessed People of the Holy Books, there is also a severe penalty for those who do evil deeds as a way of life. They must know that the divine knowledge cannot be dictated or forced upon others or be the source of discrimination, instead it has to be practically demonstrated by them with good deeds and due regards for the whole of humanity. I can therefore define in just a few words, the followers of the Holy Books are supposed to be, 'The humble people always mindful of God,' a symbol of patience and tolerance, race with each other to win the competition of treating all humans kindly and justly regardless of religion or no religion, protecting the animals from cruelty, and protecting the environment. Failing which, they need to get back to the very basics of their Holy Books for guidance to fulfil the very basic commandment of God, and to realise that, 'The Higher You Go, The Harder You Fall.'

Towards the end, I will draw your kind attention to a verse of the Holy Qur'an, as below:

'He has sent down the Book to you. Some verses are precise in meaning, which are the essence of the Book: and the other verses are allegorical. Only God knows the true meanings.' **(Qur'an 3:7)**

You must have noticed that, the verse Qur'an 5:48, has a pivotal role in my book which I have explained it in great details in the overall context of the Holy Qur'an to the best of my honesty as I understand it. However, if someone thinks that Judaism, Christianity or Islam is the only religion acceptable to God, than even part of this verse would suffice as, 'race to do good, you will all return to God and He will make clear to you the matters you used to dispute about,' hence it upholds the purpose and title of my book, 'Christians and Muslims, race to do good.' The choice is entirely yours.

Strategy of Friendship Between the Christians and Muslims

The history has sadly witnessed our ancestors (Jews, Christians and Muslims), bless them all, who tried to resolve their differences with their gloves off, and bruised each other. Let us try to create a culture of learning to differ for our future generations, race to do good to serve the humanity, and be a role model for the world. There are much better, more exciting and noble things to do, like to reach those who are suffering. I have provisionally listed below some combined ventures to be deliberated through seminars and mutual discussions at all levels. An individual, a family, a street, a community, and all other communities make our world, and working together for a noble cause makes our world beautiful for all, regardless of race, religion or colour. To start with, let us make our streets safe and pleasant. In order to serve the humanity, we do not need a leader to lead or mislead us, or guide or misguide us, we need sincere and positive attitudes and God will lead and guide us.

Combined Ventures. It is good to realise the true feelings of the people who are faced with hunger, injustice, corruption, suppression, exploitation, police high-handedness, slavery, discrimination of women, mothers having no milk to breast feed their children, child labour, and forceful occupations are a few to mention. Forceful occupations are extremely painful for the victims, who are hoping for God fearing people to rescue them. It is also important to realise the feelings and sufferings of the animals who are in our control and are suffering cruelty in

158

the hands of cruel people. Many governments have enslaved the minds of their people and reduced them to nothing more than finding bread for today. They are supported by hypocrites, whereas many God fearing people and the victims in that society are helpless. To campaign for the relief of the sufferings of animals and humans will please God and bring His blessings to all of us for this world and the world hereafter. Charity alone is not the solution to problems, as most of it goes into the hands of corrupt officials. The permanent solution lies in the freedom, and the provisions of basic human rights to all people to lead their lives in peace and dignity. Therefore we need to raise the level, to give a severe warning and ultimatum to such governments, that the vulnerable are no more alone at their mercy, we are with them day in and day out as brothers in humanity to restore their dignity, to get them their basic human rights and justice. It will provide hope to the vulnerable as well as God fearing people in the community through peaceful means like the recent example of the Egyptian people to get rid of the crooked and corrupt rulers who had suppressed their own people.

I started writing this book about a year ago to urge the Christians and Muslims to reach to those in need and in pain. I have no suitable words to express my feelings about the military response by the international community against the Libyan regime to protect killing of the innocent civilians, who were simply asking for their basic human rights. While I appreciate it, I also wonder, is it the right solution where the cause of the problem is not being addressed, which is the dictator and his inner circle of beneficiaries. Maybe, those who are supporting the regime are also victims and helpless, being driven by the cruel system out of fear for their survival. The permanent solution therefore lies to go back to our Holy

Books for guidance, where the people are to be judged by their righteous deeds. The democratic reforms are the tried, tested and the best solution for the people to determine their own future, if followed in its true spirit. States and civil societies must create a culture of **race to do good**, to serve the humanity, restore their dignity and provide justice. The safety of the people, particularly of minorities, should be the integral part of the constitution of a state, and enforceable by United Nations. The law enforcing agencies in such troubled countries, including the head of the state, must take an oath in public not to indulge in corruption and use of excessive force against innocent civilians under any circumstances. The international community needs to put a world order in place to avoid it happening, rather than to kill some people while trying to protect others as a last resort.

In order to accomplish this mission, all the communities must also have a laugh and fun together, by participating in various joint activities of entertainment, sports, social, academic, other fields, and learn good things from each other. Old people are like a library and a golden opportunity for us to learn from their experience, by involving them in joint activities where possible before it is too late. Surely without the active participation of women and children, a society can never ever be classified as a complete society.

Note. If you feel that, this book will help to understand each other and work together to serve the humanity, you may like to recommend it to others. Visit www.racetodogood.co.uk

Let us together pray for all. May I request you to join me to pray to God for His blessings and mercy for all, regardless of any race, religion, colour or gender, and urge them to, **'race to do good.'**